Procurement Marketing
A Strategic Concept

Springer
Berlin
Heidelberg
New York
Barcelona
Budapest
Hong Kong
London
Milan
Paris
Singapore
Tokyo

Udo Koppelmann

Procurement Marketing

A Strategic Concept

Translated by
Alex Lüders, P&L TRANSLATIONS

With 92 Figures

 Springer

Author

Prof. Dr. Udo Koppelmann
University of Cologne
Seminar für Allg. Betriebswirtschaftslehre,
Beschaffung und Produktpolitik
Herbert-Lewin-Str. 2
D-50931 Cologne
Germany

Translator

Alex Lüders
P&L TRANSLATIONS
Liebigstraße 52
D-60323 Frankfurt am Main
Germany

The original book as well as the present translation were realized in cooperation
with Bundesverband Materialwirtschaft, Einkauf und Logistik e.v. (BME), i.e. the
German Association for Materials Management, Purchasing and Logistics.

ISBN 3-540-64459-8 Springer-Verlag Berlin Heidelberg New York Tokyo

Cataloging-in-Publication Data applied for
Die Deutsche Bibliothek – CIP-Einheitsaufnahme
Koppelmann, Udo:
Procurement marketing : a strategic concept / Udo Koppelmann. Transl.
by Alex Lüders. - Berlin ; Heidelberg ; New York ; Barcelona ; Budapest ;
Hong Kong ; London ; Milan ; Paris ; Singapore ; Tokyo : Springer, 1998
 ISBN 3-540-64459-8

© Springer-Verlag Berlin · Heidelberg 1998
Printed in Germany

Hardcover-Design: Erich Kirchner, Heidelberg

SPIN 10656104   42/2202-5 4 3 2 1 0 – Printed on acid-free paper

Preamble

Companies with a vision have realized long ago that the procurement function can contribute considerably to securing competitive advantages and improving corporate results. Sophisticated procurement marketing is essential for meeting every-day requirements in purchasing and procurement.

For more than 40 years, the German Association for Materials Management, Purchasing and Logistics (Bundesverband Materialwirtschaft, Einkauf und Logistik e.V. - BME) has actively supported information flow and higher levels of proficiency in the field of materials management, purchasing and logistics.

With the present book Professor Koppelmann and the BME want to encourage all those interested in the field to consider new approaches and strategic solutions in purchasing and procurement.

We would like to thank Professor Koppelmann for this exceptional work. Moreover, acknowledgements are due to all those involved in the realization of the original book as well as the present translation.

Frankfurt, January 1997
Dr. Holger Hildebrandt
Chairman of the board
Bundesverband Materialwirtschaft, Einkauf und Logistik e.V.

Author's note

Procurement marketing is more than a business buzzword. It is a new strategic concept with enormous potentials for the corporate added-value chain. The discussion about procurement marketing could fill many a page and many a book. Most people lack the time for comprehensive reading on theoretical and strategical procurement subjects, however.

When the chairman of the Bundesverband Materialwirtschaft, Einkauf und Logistik e.V, Dr. Holger Hildebrandt, asked me whether the core aspects of procurement marketing could be compiled in a way which would allow an easier translation of relevant theoretical findings into every-day business, I tool the challenge. In cooperation with the renown German publishing house Springer and the German Association for Materials Management, Purchasing and Logistics (BME) the book was first published in German and then translated into English by Alex Lüders, of P&L Translations.

We hope that the present book will prove to be a valuable tool for your every-day business.

Cologne, January 1998   Udo Koppelmann

Table of Contents

1. Problems

Complaints are part of every-day business. Companies always find reasons to complain, even when they are doing well. But look at the bright side of it, at least this gives you the chance to change things. And you will find that people are more inclined to consider changes when they are not satisfied with a situation. In Materials Management this translates into reevaluating existing attitudes and approaches in order to contribute more to corporate success. Faced with this task it will not suffice to carry on whingeing about an all-too limited room for manoeuvre, particularly as people tend to create such limitations themselves. With this book we would like to encourage changes. But why should you take the risk?

1.1 Corporate Problems

World-wide competition has changed and become more fierce in recent years. Basically, there is not only everything but too much of everything. What we are witnessing today are the effects of global competition. Even companies in niche markets are forced to operate on a global scale. Global corporate activities, however, require global supply structures.

In the past, technological leadership used to ensure a company´s monopolistic position in a market. Today, a considerable number of serious competitors are emerging from quickly industrializing countries like, e.g., South Korea. Companies in these countries benefit from cost structures which are totally different from those in the Western world. Moreover, they are quickly gaining ground by using new information technology and world-wide information networks. Many established international companies find it difficult to catch up with today´s young and progressive companies.

In this environment a number of problems have arisen which have considerable consequences for the corporate supply situation.

(1) The cost problem

Cheaper competitors force companies world-wide to cut costs. But this is easier said than done. It is a fact that labour costs in countries like Germany, for example, are higher than in other countries. And there is not much a single company can do about it. The same applies to currency fluctuations. Although you could increase your purchasing activities in countries with recently devaluated currencies, the question is for how long you would be able to gain from such devaluations. How soon will the effects of a devaluation be outbalanced by an increasing rate of inflation? And as far as global sourcing is concerned, do not forget how much it costs to find and develop new suppliers in foreign countries and the risks you may be taking in the process.

Favourable offers from quickly industrializing countries can lead to a reorganization and relocation of complete production processes in the Western part of the world. In spite of the indisputable risks involved, the benefits to be gained from the opening of the former Eastern European countries, e.g., have made a great number of companies consider the relocation of some of their labour-intensive production processes to countries like the Czech Republic or Poland.

Other strategies are aimed at the reduction of internal costs. Concepts like "Lean Management" and "Business Reengineering" have been implemented in many companies. Moreover, a new network approach in optimizing processes has been widely used by companies world-wide to secure competitive advantages.

As a consequence of the increasingly pressing need to reduce internal costs the corporate procurement function has considerably grown in importance.

(2) The price problem

What price can you get for a product or service nowadays? The old days when we used to increase prices by 20 to 30 per cent every time we launched a new or follow-up product are long gone. Target pricing requires target costing. After finding out which prices are offered by competitors and establishing the price behaviour of a specific target group, a price is fixed which is believed to be realistic. This price is then used as a basis for calculating how much every single component of a product is allowed to costs. Such an approach, however, can cause major cost and price problems. Another problem is that customers have become more price conscious. Even top products are struggling to achieve top price levels today. Only high quality and special services can justify above average prices. It has become one of the main tasks of the procurement function to search globally for sources which can supply components and services at prices which will help maintain a company´s price levels. This crucial procurement task could be regarded as a preliminary stage of product development and design.

(3) The time problem

World-wide, many established companies find it increasingly hard to catch up with young and progressive companies. We have already said that. Saying it is one thing though, acting accordingly something completely different. Just take a look around. You will find more examples for ways things should not be done than for ways they should be done.

In the mid-80s, Porter introduced the terms *production processes* and *corporate added value chain*, thus starting off many a rationalization project in the industry. A similar approach for the trade sector had already been developed by Seyffert in the 1930s. As both trade and industry want to develop and launch their new products and services quicker than their competitors, a lot of companies in the industrial sector could easily have adopted that approach then. Fearful hesitation and statements like "Are you sure about that? - But we have never done it that way" stopped them. This way of thinking, however, has never marked a winner. Without "me too" products you will never be able to make "me too" profits.

It is becoming increasingly difficult to keep up with developments without taking chances. Unless you want to be stuck with the old ways of doing things, you will have to take risks. This will trigger major changes in the procurement function. Repetitive procedures and standard order fulfillment will continue to lose in importance.

(4) The innovation problem

The necessity to come up with new ideas is indisputable. Future competition will not simply be about products but innovations. This, however, will call for creativity, lean management and empowerment on all corporate levels. In future, you will only earn more money if you can find new and better ways of doing things. Traditional adminis-trative materials management will be replaced by entrepreneurial procurement mar-keting.

4

(5) The acceptance problem

Anything a company does affects its image one way or the other. It does not go unnoticed how a company treats the environment, its staff, customers and suppliers. And it does not really make any difference whether the public is actually being fair or unfair in its judgement of a company's operations - just take the conflict between Greenpeace and Shell over the oil platform Brent Spar as an example.

It is essential, however, that you know how to handle information, e.g., when you are working on a process optimization project and you need your supplier's cost calculations for a total cost analysis. Information provided confidentially must never be abused. A common tactic is to request quotations for large order volumes in order to be offered the lowest possible prices and then to place much smaller orders. Yet another tactic is to aks for an overall price reduction of 10 per cent claiming that prices had been far too high in the past.

If you want to establish customer-supplier relationships based on trust and cooperation, such purchasing techniques are hardly appropriate. Power games will not provide you with long-term solutions. Only a strategical, cooperative approach will help you deal with the multitude of problems which can arise in procurement.

1.2 Procurement Problems

The corporate supply situation is changing, thus causing major problems beyond the traditional boundaries of single corporate functions.

(1) Lack of acceptance

The corporate procurement (purchasing / buying) function is a mediator between the internal customer and the external supplier. Requirements of various corporate functions have to be satisfied. In a lot of companies, however, the procurement function is still merely fulfilling orders instead of actively trying to influence corporate demands. Purchasing departments are often limited to selecting suitable sources of supply and negotiating the commercial side of contracts according to the instructions of the R+D or construction departments. You will find that staff who have so far only been al-

lowed to follow instructions need time to learn how to actively influence demands
with a view to achieving previously defined targets.

(2) Lack of strategy

The fulfillment of orders requires an operative-tactical approach. Illustration 1 shows a
clear focus on materials planning and scheduling.

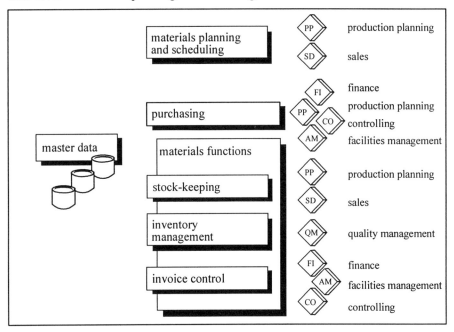

Illustration 1: Materials plannning with SAP R/3

Strategies, however, call for long-term planning. A survey which was recently conducted in Germany showed that only 24 per cent of all companies questioned have
long-term plans for their materials supply. A strategical approach is clearly lacking
here.

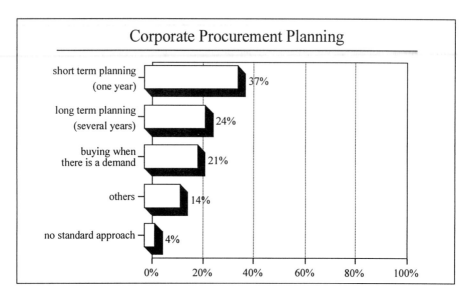

Illustration 2: Materials planning in German companies (see Industrieller Einkauf heute, without named author, Beschaffung aktuell, 12/95, p.25.)

How can a corporate function expect to be taken seriously if it can only provide short-term plans?

(3) Lack of methods

The above mentioned survey also included questions about the purchasing methods most commonly used in German companies (see Illustration 3).

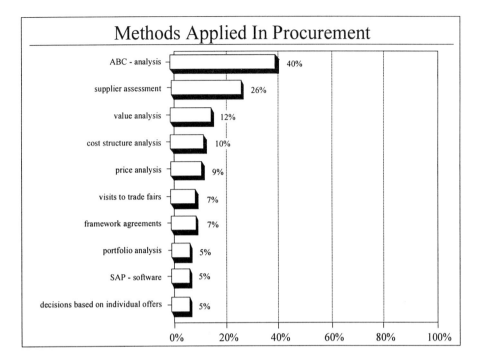

Illustration 3: Purchasing methods used in German companies

The variety of methods and tools used in a corporate function illustrates its state-of-the-art. You will find it difficult, however, to speak of any state-of-the-art when looking at the results of the survey. The placement of job orders, the implementation of SAP-software, the negotiation of framework agreements or the evaluation of suppliers may be standard purchasing tasks but can hardly be described as strategical methods of procurement.

(4) Lack of trust

Here they are, purchaser and supplier facing each other at the negotiating table, thinking that anything that may be of advantage to one party must automatically be a disadvantage for the other. Trying to pull your supplier over the table while secretly hoping that he will somehow manage to do the same to your competitors is a more common practice than you might think. This way of dealing with your supplier, however, is hardly compatible with process-oriented strategies like system sourcing, simultaneous engineering, etc. And the breaking up of the partnership is merely a question of time.

(5) Lack of know-how

You have learned your trade and surely acquired considerable expertise over the years. However, if you want to contribute to the identification of new solutions for your company, you will need to acquire additional know-how. Otherwise you might find it very difficult to understand the new network approaches and comprehensive concepts in today's business. The new ways of realizing supplier evaluation projects or gathering valuable information, for example, may remain a mystery to you.

(6) Lack of competence

As long as purchasers are only executing other people's instructions it is not surprising that the procurement function still has a "middleman" image rather than being accepted as an important and highly competent management function. Any ideas coming from that corner - as good as they may be - tend to be met with reluctance. Moreover, technical engineers have been widely known to influence the supply process directly by negotiating with suppliers or, indirectly, by asking for specific suppliers in their materials requirement forms. All parties involved in the supply process have to realize, however, that it is the purchaser who has the expertise and thorough knowledge of markets and suppliers which places him in a position to achieve the best possible supply solutions for a company. Understanding this is a learning process to which the present book wants to contribute.

2. The Vision

For achieving a higher level of professionalism in a corporate function it is essential to set some targets first. Which qualifications, e.g., does a procurement manager need in order to fulfil his tasks to the full satisfaction of his company? Which abilities does he require to master procurement problems? Depending on the current state of development in your company, you will either read the vision described in this chapter with disbelief or greet it with approval. While there are certainly many companies which have already made great progress in their professional development, there are even more which are only just starting to realize the need to change their attitudes and procedures. And you would not believe how many companies are still completely ignorant of the fact that changes are necessary in the first place.

2.1 The Theory

Economic theories and principles can be extremely useful in every-day business. Theories are usually based on real cases and situations, however, they abstract from reality by focusing on core issues and leaving out anything that is marginal and not important. When theories prove to be right in their interpretation of reality, they can provide you with a valuable set of truths. In procurement this is the more important as people tend to have more confidence in new approaches when they are based on accepted theories.

Moreover, theories provide structures which reflect real life. In an increasingly confusing world, structures can provide guidance and help us to focus on what is essential. They encourage deductive learning processes. In other words, people who lack theoretical knowledge are often so used to the way things have traditionally been done in their companies that they find it difficult to work for other companies or operate in new markets. Although inductive learning is certainly valuable, misinterpretations and mistakes happen more easily.

The visions described in this chapter are based on two theories which will be explained in the following:

2.11 The Coalition Theory

In the mid-50s, a new theory on corporate behaviour was developed in the USA (Simon, 1955; March/Simon, 1958; Cybert/March, 1963). According to this theory a company is an open social system (see Illustration 4).

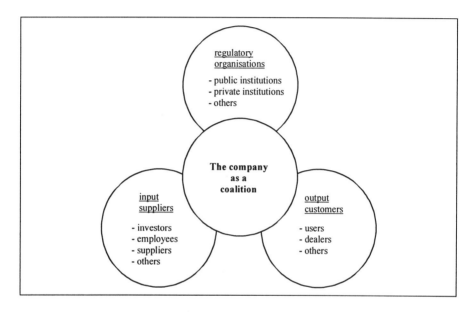

Illustration 4: The company as a coalition

The system works like a political coalition. This means that a company can only prosper as long as all parties involved feel that they are getting a fair share for the work and efforts they are putting into the company. Their reward can be payment, social acceptance, further training or career prospects. People who feel that their company is taking advantage and is not offering them any future will soon start looking for another job. But it is usually only the most talented people in whom companies invest money for training and personal development. These employees naturally have better chances to get new jobs than staff who have lower qualifications or are of a more advanced age. The latter often prefer to keep their heads down and very often reduce both their input and their commitment to far below the required standards. No company can survive this in the long run.

This theory on the internal workings of a company can also be applied to the relationships between a company and its environment. Let us focus on supplier relationships here. Buying and supplying companies also form coalitions. Such coalitions, however, can only work as long as all parties involved have the feeling that they are treated correctly. Anybody who feels being taken advantage of will, sooner or later, act accordingly.

A supplier who is forced to sell his product below cost price will seek to find a way to reduce costs by cutting on materials costs or quality standards. Moreover, he will start to put all his efforts in more profitable orders. He might even turn out to be less reliable and be hardly open to customer requests for adjustments in quantities, time or quality, let alone for additional investments. On the other hand, any buyer who feels that he or she is being pulled over the table will try to find other, more trustworthy and cooperative sources of supply.

Once the equilibrium within the coalition is disturbed, the parties will start looking for new problems instead of looking for solutions. When this happens, partnerships normally do not last very long.

12

2.12 Incentive-Contribution-Theory

The incentive-contribution theory is based on the coalition theory. Illustration 5 shows how both buyer and supplier are trying to find out what the other party wants and what it is prepared to give.

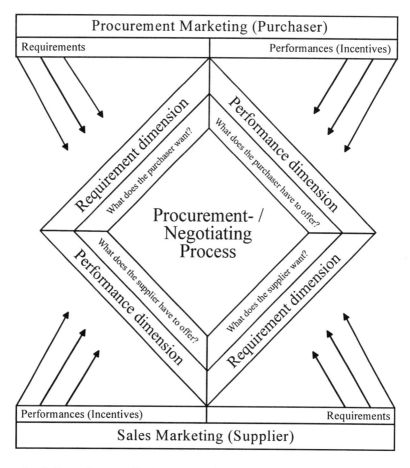

Illustration 5: Incentive-contribution concept in procurement

Buyers always try to get anything at rock-bottom prices. However, they have to offer their supplier something in return. This adds up to a simple economic calculation (see Illustration 6).

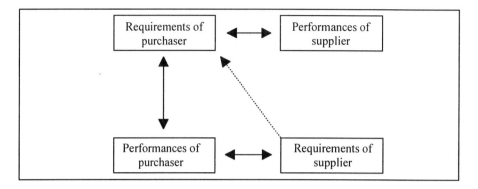

Illustration 6: Factors of the incentive-contribution theory

Illustration 6 proves that it is not sufficient to see your own requirements, on the one hand, and your supplier's performances, on the other. The new approach is essentially based on the idea that you have to try and find out what you can offer your supplier in return for his delivering your order at rock-bottom prices. Focusing on the price alone does not suffice. It is important for a buyer to develop an understanding for the needs and problems of his suppliers and to find ways to meet their needs. However, to make the calculation viable, it is essential that you understand your own cost structures and consider internal cost reductions as well. Hardly anybody does this though.

2.2 Consequences of the Vision

Whingeing will not get you anywhere. We have already established that. It is not only the management which has to realize the many opportunities that professional procurement management offers. Procurement staff need to understand themselves how their profession will change in the future and what kind of consequences for the corporate supply chain this might have.

14

2.21 Changes in Attitudes

Corporate materials management has to undergo fundamental changes.

(1) Win-win

The coalition theory proves that win-lose approaches disrupt the economic equilibrium. When looking for your benefits in a deal you must always remember the benefits for your supplier. If he does not like certain parts of a deal, you must try to make them more attractive to him. Trying to think of compromises which are satisfactory for both parties before actually entering into contract negotiations will make the subsequent negotiations much more transparent and easier to conduct. The parties to the contract need a variety of efficient tools and methods. Win-win situations can only be established if these tools are used in a much more sophisticated way then in the past. But we will come back to this later.

When implementing new purchasing strategies you are most likely to start with your most important suppliers. The fewer suppliers you have, the easier this will be. You can, e.g., outsource the procurement of your C-parts to an external purchasing office. The efforts you have to put into creating win-win situations here will be justified by the elimination of many internal processes.

Win-win strategies have to replace the power-oriented policy of single-mindedly enforcing demands. Power politics usually result in a concentration of the supplier base and, eventually, in an equilibrium of powers. The best process improvements can be achieved through cooperation. The supplier must understand the importance of his own win-position in the future. You will achieve far better results by convincing your supplier of potential advantages for him than by putting him under pressure.

(2) Process orientation

Like any entrepreneurial activity, procurement too is characterized by the quest for cost reductions and the improvement of performances, i.e. the two basic components of free market economy. When seeking to optimize activities it is crucial to look at complete processes rather than isolated process factors. The cost price, e.g., is certainly an important factor in a purchase decision, but you have to consider both the cost of the purchase object itself and the cost of the procurement process (sourcing and processing costs for example). The latter can considerably increase a purchase price which at first glance may seem favourable. Ordering materials of higher quality can reduce the likelihood of having to complain about poor quality or even having to pay for repairs.

Process orientation does not only affect procurement. Unless you look at complete processes including sales planning, product design, production, logistics and procurement, you will find it difficult to achieve satisfactory solutions. Moreover, the process chain has to be extended beyond the boundaries of your company. This calls for cooperation on a vertical and horizontal level. Vertical cooperation defines the processes between buyer and supplier. Product designers of the supplying and the buying company, e.g., can work together on product improvements. Cooperation between two companies can encompass all corporate functions on all process levels, i.e. teams of both the buying and the selling company get together to find solutions which are mutually satisfactory. Isolated steps are thus replaced by comprehensive solutions.

Process orientation requires a network approach as well as team work. All team members need to see beyond the traditional boundaries of their respective functions. This approach has a number of advantages:

- Provided that teamwork is prepared and managed professionally, the decision making process is shortened. Instead of isolated planning and subsequently having to take corrective measures, important decisions are discussed and agreed upon together.
- The quality of the decision-making process is improved when isolated approaches are replaced by network approaches. Solutions which from your point of view may seem second-best can actually turn out to be the better solutions when considering their long-term effects. This is something you might realize after having had the chance to look at things from other people's points of view.
- The cost of the decision-making process is reduced as time is saved and fewer corrective measures are necessary.

16

Illustration 7 shows a possible way of cooperation between two companies.

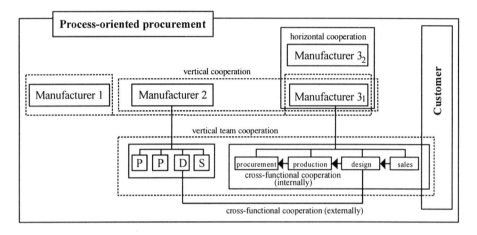

Illustration 7: Process-oriented procurement

(3) Strategic focus

When preparing important long-term deals you must not get distracted by tactical or operative tasks. It is imperative that you try to delegate as much of your operative daily business as possible. If your company has decided to concentrate on its core business, so should the individual corporate functions. You have to decide what is important in your business and what is not. And bear in mind that whatever you decide today will have consequences in future. If you antagonize your suppliers today, they are not likely to forget it tomorrow. Changing your supplier every time you find a cheaper one might seem clever at the time. But do not forget about the long-term consequences of such a behaviour. Global sourcing, e.g., can be a costly thing. And changing your supply market is risky business. Make sure the benefits to be gained by your company are higher than the risks and costs involved.

Only an intensive analysis of vertical and horizontal processes and procedures in your company will enable you to make full use of all the opportunities arising from the realization of process orientation. The selection of system suppliers must be considered from a strategic point of view. This does not only require a thorough analysis of potential suppliers but also the cultivation of existing supplier relationships. Everybody on the sales side knows how important it is to look after your customer and increase customer satisfaction. Key supplier management in purchasing, however, is almost unheard of.

Strategic thinking requires the ability to anticipate developments. It is not enough to follow trends. What kind of results can be achieved through buying abroad and what kind of problems could arise? You cannot possibly start to source globally and expect that everything is going to run smoothly right from the word go without any major internal and external adjustments.

(4) Service orientation

The internal purchasing function is a mediating function. In order to satisfy internal demands external sources have to be identified. As far as this is concerned the purchasing function resembles a trading function, with the main target being the satisfaction of customer demands with suitable products. Moreover, in trading companies, the purchasing and sales functions have to cooperate closely in order to secure corporate success: securing the company´s retail prices is a crucial criterion for the purchasing department. In the industrial sector, the purchasing function should also remember that, in the end of the day, it is the sales figures which are the evidence of successful purchasing. Purchasing provides valuable customer services and is not simply the executor of instructions given by other corporate functions like R+D, product design or construction. Cross-functional teams must focus on how to gain benefits for the end customer.

Purchasing has to provide services for two types of customers, the more important of which is the end customer. It is essential that purchasing is included in the early process of deciding what the end customer needs and what he is prepared to pay. Only then is the purchasing function in a position to work with other corporate functions on viable compromises for the supply of materials required for production. And only then can the purchaser search for creative, strategic supply solutions. If you provide services for other departments you need background information on factors like production costs, performance levels and productivity. Otherwise you will find it difficult to

realize cost reductions by suggesting alternative materials, let alone by identifying re-
design potentials.

Moreover, it is the task of the purchaser to make sure that internal materials demands
are fulfilled. Win-win situations with suppliers have to be established. This is hardly
possible if suppliers are changed frequently. Business partners who remember how
they solved problems in the past will find it easier to tackle similar problems in the
future. This does not mean that you should abandon your search for better suppliers.
Before you start any global sourcing projects, however, you should work out what you
want to achieve and what price you are prepared to pay. Even in companies which
have a clear global sourcing strategy, sourcing costs are often disguised in the over-
heads instead of being allocated clearly to individual projects. And risks regarding
quality, quantity, delivery time and process costs are seldom considered when changing suppliers.

(5) Teamwork

Lean management calls for well selected and qualified staff as they do not need to be
controlled but are capable of managing themselves. Empowerment means that tasks
are delegated and management control is limited to a minimum. These are crucial pre-
requisits for successful team work and optimum results. Your efforts must not focus on
what your superior might say but on what the best long-term solutions will be.

Once team work has been established you can gradually start to replace traditional
ways of successive planning by simultaneous planning methods. On a team there have
to be specialists from sales, design, purchasing, logistics, production or finance who
are responsible for particular parts of the project while other parts of the project should
remain the responsibility of specialized corporate functions. Teamwork has two targets:

– to achieve optimum results within the shortest possible time. When different corporate functions work successively on different parts of a project too much time is
lost. Project work is hardly efficient when purchasing departments have to postpone
their sourcing activities until construction and production have finally given their

go ahead and sales and product management have completed their market evaluations.

- to achieve better solutions by discussing problems in teams rather than making isolated decisions.

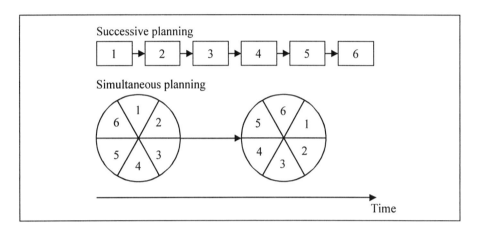

Illustration 8: Successive planning versus simultaneous planning

These targets define the skills required by members of a team:

- Team members need to be experts in their respective fields. They have to be able to work with highly qualified and specialized people. Purchasers whose expertise is limited to the acquisition of electrical materials, e.g., will struggle to work in teams of highly qualified staff from marketing, production, construction, logistics, and finance. Purchasers do not only have to know their markets thoroughly, they also have to be able to recognize potentials for redesigning products and optimizing production processes.

- Teamwork requires an open mind and flexibility. If you are not up-to-date with recent developments in your field, you might not be considered to be competent for the task and find it hard to get the necessary support for your ideas and suggestions. Teams have to focus on discussing comprehensive, overall solutions rather than looking into the details of a problem. Insisting on your point of view without listening to the arguments of your fellow team members will impede team success.

On the quest for optimum overall solutions the purchaser needs to be able to offer a wide range of alternatives.

- In successful teams all team members have learned to think along the lines of their fellow team members. They have developed an understanding for each other's points of view. The more alike people are in their ways of thinking, the easier they find it to convince each other of their respective points of view.

- A certain degree of selfconfidence on part of individual team members is not necessarily a disadvantage as long as an equilibrium of powers can be maintained. It is necessary to make sure, however, that there are no antagonisms among the team members which could impede team success.

- Teamwork requires a high degree of disciplin on part of the team members. A growing room for manoeuvre increases the risk of wasted resources. Team members tend to get sidetracked in discussions and details which are of no consequence to the task at hand. It is important to concentrate on core tasks. Disciplin is essential when targets have to be met and time fences observed. In every team meeting the individual team members are given tasks which have to be fulfilled by the next meeting. As the exact dates of the team meetings are usually fixed well in advance there is no excuse for wasting everybody's time and money by going into a meeting unprepared. In that case the complete teamwork might have to be rescheduled and decisions postponed.

2.22 Visions of Organisation

A materials management function which has to report to production or finance several levels further up in the corporate hierarchy is hardly in a good position for suggesting creative and innovative ideas for the optimization of products and processes. This is a problem that must be addressed without delay.

(1) Procurement as a market-oriented function

Procurement and sales have much in common. While sales activities focus on the end customer, procurement strategies concentrate on the supplier. Key account management aims at utmost customer satisfaction by providing comprehensive services. Modular sourcing, on the other hand, is a strategy that requires continuous cooperation with your supplier in order to identify problems before they actually arise and find mutually satisfactory solutions. A similar way of thinking is therefore the basis for successful cooperation between purchasing and sales.

Another argument in favour of stronger cooperation between the two functions is the world-wide market presence which most sales functions have established long before the procurement functions even started thinking about going international. It is far less expensive to let purchasers use sales facilities and the expertise of a company's international sales representatives than to establish separate purchasing offices abroad. Sales offices in foreign markets are in a position to gather procurement-related information and include them in their country reports without major additional costs.

Another reason for the sales and purchasing functions having to cooperate more closely in the future is that some of their business partners may, at the same time, be their customer and supplier. Horizontal and vertical cooperation is to create dense corporate networks. As a consequence, procurement will not operate without sales nor sales without procurement in the future.

(2) Procurement marketing and logistics

There are many reasons for separating procurement marketing from the physical flow of materials. The first and foremost task of procurement is to negotiate with suppliers, deal with general supply questions and find solutions for meeting internal demands when they arise. Logistics activities, on the other hand, start after an order has been placed. In most companies, materials planning and scheduling, inventory management and transport are still responsibilities of the procurement function. When implementing comprehensive PPS systems, however, it is more reasonable to delegate the complete materials planning and scheduling, including inventory management and transport, to a logistics function. Procurement marketing and logistics differ greatly in their approaches and way of thinking. While the purchasing function should focus on mediating between internal customer and external supplier, logistics functions should manage other links in the supply chain.

(3) Procurement as profit centre

Not only companies which operate worldwide need to check the performance levels of individual corporate functions in order to allocate responsibilities to the function which is best suited for a job. Also companies with only one production site need to know how efficient their procurement function is.

There are several possibilities for measuring performances. Companies can work with key figures or try benchmarking. Profit centres can decide themselves which goods and services they want to purchase for internal customers, which ones for external customers, and which procurement tasks should better be outsourced.

Organizing procurement as a profit centre can also settle the ongoing dispute about the centralisation or decentralisation of procurement. If a local purchasing department can procure materials or services better and cheaper than the "central" profit centres, it can credit itself with the additional profits. At a later stage it might be well worth a thought to transform such a procurement profit centre into an independent legal entity. The establishment of a "Purchasing and Trading Service" would be the final step of service orientation.

(4) Allocation of new responsibilities

Highly complex procurement systems and objects call for the allocation of new responsibilities for purchasing professionals.

The main task of the new *Supply Requirement Manager* is to solve internal problems in the creation and identification of corporate requirements. Such a central function is especially useful in large industrial groups where the coordination between the production sites, divisions and branches is the more difficult, the more different their production environments and work conditions are.

The main responsibility of the new *Supplier Relationship Manager* is to solve external conflicts. He has to make sure that mutually defined conditions are fullfilled to the complete satisfaction of all parties involved. Moreover, he has to act on behalf of the purchaser when identifying potential supply problems as early as possible and initiating appropriate steps.

Both the *Supply Requirement Manager* and the *Supplier Relationship Manager* have to use sophisticated information and communication technology in order to address problems wherever they arise without delay. For that task they have to be available at all times.

The *Information Manager* has to provide all the information required for decision-making processes in procurement. Information is a vital prerequisite for professional international sourcing even though many companies still do not seem to have realized that. There are various aspects which need to be taken into consideration:

– It has to be established which information is required in the first place. In the process of evaluating markets and suppliers the *Information Manager* might gather a lot of additional information but it is essential that the team members stipulate which information is actually relevant for their projects.

– It has to be decided where and how information is to be gathered. Where and at what cost can up-to date, comprehensive information be obtained and which methods can be used to achieve optimum results? This means that the *Information Manager* needs to know how to use the tools and methods available for the collection of relevant data.

– It has to be ensured that the information which has been gathered can actually be used by purchasing staff. The ability to design an information system which, on the one hand, encourages staff to use the system for reference and, on the other hand, provides individuals with the information they need for a specific project reflects the professional competence of the *Information Manager*.

3. Possible Solutions

For a better understanding of the solutions offered in chapter 4.0 it may be useful to consider certain aspects of the problems first.

3.1 Why Procurement Marketing?

Marketing and materials management differ considerably in their approaches and ways of thinking. This is one of the reasons why they have different positions within the corporate hierarchy.

Marketing originates from the marketing of consumer products for profit-oriented commercial enterprises, i.e. from sales-oriented product marketing. This approach has been widely used and adopted by both the service and trade sector. The marketing of industrial goods followed suit. As early as 1972 did Kotler point out that marketing strategies could be adopted by other functions as well. His concept of generic marketing eventually lead to non-profit marketing (marketing for non-profit organisations and charities) as well as procurement marketing (see *Buying is marketing too*, 1972). This had major consequences in many organisations world-wide. Raffée explained in 1979:"By conducting in a market business transactions with business partners, be it suppliers, workers or investors, a company secures the resources it needs for generating and utilizing performances. As sales and purchasing activities share a number of similar problems and targets it seems logical to apply the marketing approach to supply market activities. The results are procurement marketing, personnel marketing and finance marketing.

Marketing is an exchange process:

- Marketing concentrates on identifying and solving (customer) problems, i.e. the problems of other parties.
- Marketing solves other parties´ problems in order to achieve its own goals.
- The more efforts are being put into addressing customer problems, the easier it is to realize marketing targets.

Procurement marketing has to deal with two kinds of customers, i.e. the internal and the external customer. This makes procurement marketing more difficult than sales or product marketing.

The emphasis on establishing reciprocative exchange processes in purchasing marketing originates from both the coalition and the incentive-contribution theory. Satisfying long-term solutions can only be achieved through fair play.

Biergans proved that generic marketing can be adopted both on a general corporate level and specifically for sales and purchasing (1984, page 92).

Generic Marketing Rules \ economic interpretation	company-specific interpretation	sales-specific interpretation (sales marketing traditional marketing)	procurement-specific interpretation (procurement marketing)
(1) Exchange process between at least two parties	Exchange process between a profit-oriented organisation and its market environment	Exchange process between a sales organisation and a buying organisation	Exchange process between a buying organisation and a supplying organisation
(2) Exchange of at least two value objects (performance objects)	Exchange of corporate performances and market performances	Exchange of supply performances of the sales organisation and counter-performances of the sales market	Exchange of requirement performances of the buying organisation and counter-performances of the supply market
(3) Search of the marketing party for a certain reaction of the other party	Search of the marketing organisation for a certain reaction on part of its market environment	Search of the marketing sales organisation for a certain reaction of the sales market	Search of the marketing buying organisation for a certain reaction of the supply market
(4) Uncertainty of getting the desired reaction from the other party	Uncertainty to get the desired reaction from the market environment	Uncertainty to get the desired reaction from the sales market	Uncertainty to get the desired reaction from the supply market
(5) Attempt of the marketing party to get the desired reaction from the other party by creating and offering values (principle of performance and counter-performance)	Attempt of the marketing party to get the desired reaction from the market environment (market performance) by creating and offering corporate performances	Attempt of the marketing sales organisation to get the desired reaction from the sales market (sales market performance) by creating and offering values (sales performance)	Attempt of the marketing buying organisation to get the desired reaction from the supply market (supply market performance) by creating and offering values (buying performance)

Illustration 9: Marketing concepts

3.2 Decision Orientation

In business administration theories there are several types of focuses when making decisions. Some experts concentrate on the links between theoretical causes, others on their reasons, and others again on the application of theories in every-day life. Making the right decision can constitute a major problem.

Decisions are characterized by several aspects:

- In a decision-making process there has to be a choice of alternatives. In chapter 4.0 we will seek to develop as many alternatives for decisions as possible.
- Any kind of decision requires assessment criteria. One of the basic criteria in business is the economic principle, i.e. the achievement of a set target with as little means as possible (minimum principle) or, respectively, the achievement of the highest possible output with the means provided (maximum principle). We will work out a variety of targets later.
- The decision-making process is not a mere input-output calulation but depends on situations and circumstances. We will look into this more closely later as well.
- When making decisions in procurement there are always uncertainties as you are dealing with people. Anticipating the way other people will act and react is extremely difficult.
- Alternatives in a decision-making process are only interesting as long as they are real options. Internal barriers within a company can limit such options considerably.
- The organization of a company can either encourage or hinder the identification of alternatives. Allocating new team responsibilities can help.
- Decison-making processes in procurement marketing are usually highly complex and insufficiently structured. The process gets the more difficult, the more parties work on different aspects of a problem over a longer period of time. Thinking processes, however, can be encouraged by structures which support decision-making processes. Splitting the complete workload into parts which complement each other establishes a thinking discipline for all parties involved and makes team work more efficient.

3.3 If-then Decisions

If you ask purchasers how they reach supply decision they will most probably tell you that "it depends" on various things. From such vague statements we can conclude:

- Procurement managers need transparent and easy procedures for making objective decisions. The target is to achieve the best possible results as quickly and economically as possible.
- If-then conditions have to be established which reflect procurement situations realistically. The purchaser needs a sophisticated choice of possible decision-making criteria. Such a choice will be developed in chapter 4.
- Suitable courses of action must be developed. Whereas if-then conditions in general can be applied on all levels of procurement marketing, the courses of actions may differ greatly on each level. We will develop a suitable model in chapter 4.0.

The definition of if-conditions - let us call them decision-making criteria - is nothing new. Ansoff developed the customer/product matrix for sales marketing in 1957. Illustration 10 shows how this matrix can be adjusted for decision-making processes in procurement.

potential suppliers / markets procurement objects	established suppliers / markets	related suppliers / markets	new suppliers / markets
established procurement objects	purely repetitive purchases consolidating relationships	modified repetitive purchases extending the supply market	supply market variation
modified procurement objects	modified repetitive purchases buying similar objects in established markets	modification in procurement (differenciation or variation)	supply market variation for modified procurement objects
new procurement objects	buying new procurement objects in established markets (procurement variation)	modification in procurement under consideration of related suppliers	procurement innovation

Illustration 10: Product/market matrix

The categories show a number of possible strategical focuses. The number of decision-making criteria, however, is limited as they are closely connected to market mechanisms. We therefore have to look for critera which influence the whole decision-making process.

In 1977, Kraljic took first steps in the right direction by defining four different types of products. Illustration 11 shows that his product types were based on the two criteria "profit" and "risk".

procurement risk \ expected profit	high	low
high	strategic products	bottleneck products
low	key products	standard products

Illustration 11: Profit/risk matrix

Kraljic used his matrix to deduct which tasks and information were of importance in purchasing. The structure of the matrix, however, does not support a consistent decision-making system.

In 1991, Scherer developed a comprehensive two-level system of elementary and supplementary criteria.

Elementary criteria can be used in decision-making situations. Every procurement object has to be assessesed according to the criteria quantity, innovation, performance level as well as singular product, standard product, established product, innovative product, top product, cheap product and purchaser-specific product.

Singular products are procurement objects which are purchased in small quantities, e.g. investment goods. Standard products, e.g. commodities, are normally standardized within a company. Established products have been purchased for a long time and are also integrated in new products. Innovative products have a high degree of novelty but may be risky. Top products have a very high performance level but tend to be more expensive than cheap products which have such a low performance level that they can be offered at low prices. Purchaser-specific products are manufactured especially for the buying company.

After having chosen from these elementary criteria, additional supplementary criteria can be selected. The criteria shown in Illustration 12 have been preselected from a great number of options.

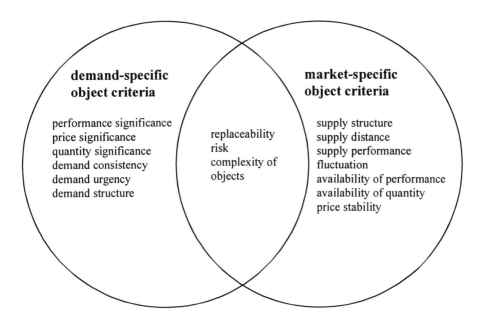

Illustration 12: Supplementary decision-making criteria

High significance of performance indicates that the purchase object is very important for the performance of the end product. High significance of price means that the purchase price strongly influences the selling price of the end product. High significance of quantity indicates that a large quantity of the purchase object is needed during each procurement period. High demand consistency originates from a XYZ analysis and re-

flects consistent quantity requirements (the x-component). The urgency of demand results from unexpected procurement situations and the cost of delayed delivery. The
demand structure can be concentrated (high share of the supply market) or concurrent
(low share of the supply market). The supply structure too can be either concentrated
or concurrent. A big supply distance means that there is a considerable geographical
distance between purchaser and supplier (global sourcing). High fluctuations in supply
performances indicate how fast purchasing objects undergo changes. The availability
of performances depends on the required performance standards. Bottlenecks in production can reduce large supply volumes even in booming markets. A high price stability is required for planning in-house costs and is therefore a highly sensitive issue.

In addition to these criteria which are closely connected to market mechanisms there
are some criteria which are clearly object-related. The possibility to replace objects
gives you more flexibility in the choice of substitute material. Highly risky purchasing
objects are either very sensitive or dangerous to the environment. A highly complex
product indicates the complexity of either its production or its application.

The above mentioned points can be used in decison-making situations
- for selecting suitable decision-making criteria,
- for assessing procurement objects,
- for categorizing the selected criteria according to their relevance,
- for determining right courses of action.

Illustration 13 gives an overview of possible courses of action in a decision-making
situation.

Condition (if-component) / Course of action (then-component)	singular product	cheap product	top product	standard product	established product	innovative product	purchaser-specific product	quantity significance (high)	performance significance (high)	price significance (high)	availability of performance (low)	others / etc.
hierarchical order			1				2					
.... requirement - supply requirements												

Illustration 13: Courses of action based on decision-making criteria

On any level of a decision-making process, special process matrixes can be designed.

Decisions in supply situations should be reached as follows:

1) The supplier does not have to fulfill general criteria but audits concentrate on the specific procurement objects the buying company actually needs. As a result the supplier evaluation is more specific and functional. Some suppliers which might not seem interesting at first might turn out to be absolutely suitable for a job.

2) After having established the possible if/then conditions for a supply situation this information should be entered in a suitable computer programme.

3) A suitable computer programme should be able to use the entered information for recommending suitable courses of action whenever similar situations reoccur.

4) A defined decision-making structure has to facilitate the quick and systematical identification of solutions.

5) Provided that all possible variances are included and explained, the computer print-out can serve as a transparent protocol. Making the right decision is thus no longer just a matter of intuition but becomes traceable and duplicable.

6) Protocols are to be used as a reference by the person initially responsible for the decision and later by those who might take over his responsibilities.

4. The Procurement Marketing Solution

The process model shown in Illustration 14 gives an overview of the different process levels in procurement marketing. They will be explained in the following.

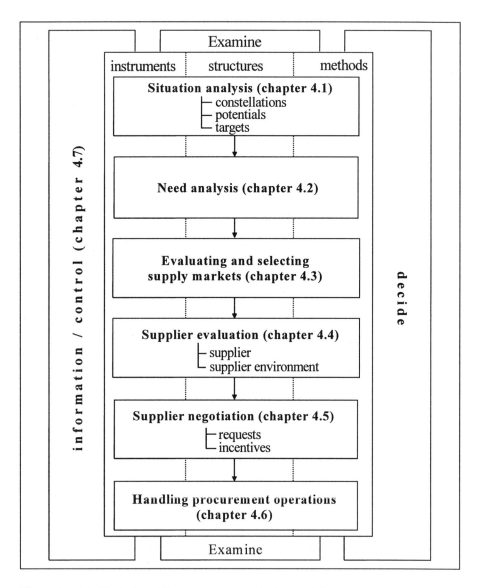

Illustration 14: The industrial procurement marketing model

Although the underlying idea of a procurement marketing model is very much the same in trade and industry, we shall focus on industrial organizations here.

4.1 Situation Analysis

Before conducting a demand analysis the decision-making environment has to be evaluated.

(1) First, it is necessary to establish which risks a company might be facing and against what kind of background procurement decisions have to be made. Secondly, an early-warning system for potential trouble has to be created in order to be able to adjust courses of action when necessary.

(2) Courses of action have to be determined by setting targets and defining strategies. The latest research in business administration can be of use here.

(3) Problems and targets have to be examined with a view to their actual potential. It is neither interesting nor viable for a company to develop any plans which have no chance of being realized in the first place.

4.11 The Room for Manoeuvre in Procurement

Circumstances and situations determine possible courses of action in procurement. This can be as much a chance as a risk for the company. Circumstances can alter quickly and unexpectedly, e.g., when an urgent demand arises in a company. Or they can change slowly, e.g., when the quality of the goods delivered by a supplier deteriorates gradually. Opportunities can arise when there is an unexpected supply situation in a market. In most cases, however, it is necessary to adjust quickly to the changed circumstances, e.g. when there is an industrial dispute. Companies need suitable adjustment plans for that kind of situation. Much more interesting for the purchasing professional are circumstances you can alter or even create yourself, for example when securing your supplier's continuous cooperation.

This means that the purchaser has to use special procurement tools systematically in

34

order to address problems efficiently and create a new quality of stability.

Illustration 15 shows different types of supply problems

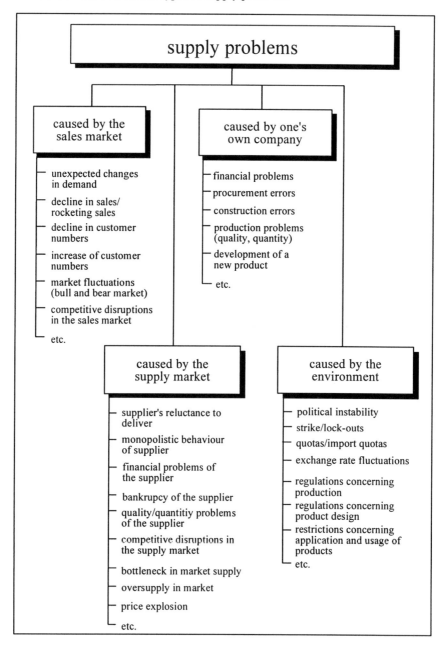

Illustration 15: Critical supply problems

Problems caused by market mechanisms are particularly important for procurement marketing.

If a potential supplier refuses to work with you, he most probably has a good reason for his decision. Has he attracted more interesting customers? Is it that you have not paid enough for his products and services? Has he been aggravated? You could ask yourself many more questions like that. Monopolistic behaviour on part of your suppliers can affect your business in many ways. You should ask yourself whether you have caused this behaviour yourself, however. Is your pricing policy, e.g., too aggressive?

The next question is what to do in that kind of situation. Would you exert pressure by trying to increase your market power or buying substitute goods and materials? This could easily backfire though. Relentless price pressure in the car industry, for example, has created monopolistic markets. Pressure politics may lead to a temporary weakening of a supplier. He may experience serious cash-flow, quality and quantity problems and even go bankrupt. But this can be as much your fault as your supplier's. Therefore, any potential problems have to be monitored and tackled as early as possible.

Moreover, you have to compete with other companies in the supply market. Your competitors might offer your suppliers more interesting strategies and tools, pay more or act and react quicker. Bottlenecks in supply emphasize this problem. Especially natural products, products dealt at the stock exchange (e.g. silver) and commodities (e.g. computer chips and control units) tend to be problematic and prone to price explosions. If an oversupply of the raw materials needed by your company causes market prices to slump, you should consider taking advantage of the situation in order to secure your company's market position. High cash-flow is a prerequisite for being able to move fast in such situations. Dealing in futures and options, on the other hand, can prevent your company from being affected by price explosions.

Illustration 16 shows possible consequences of supply problems which you can either try to avoid or use to your advantage.

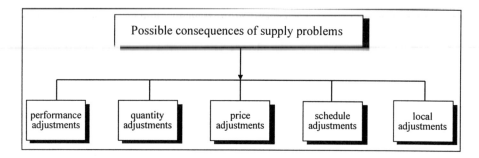

Illustration 16: Possible consequences of supply problems

(1) Performance adjustments can mean increases or decreases in performance levels as well as a new perfomance altogether. Decreases in performance levels are not desireable as they might affect the goods and services required by your company. Increases in performance levels, on the other hand, may lead to improving overall performance levels in a line of business. The first company in a position to make use of new and better performances can, at least for a while, secure a certain competitive advantage. New performances reflect altered customer demands and may consequently lead to the development of new products. Bying new products, however, initially requires considerable efforts. We will deal with this problem later.

(2) Quantity adjustments can indicate a high or low availability of a product or service. In both cases the consequences for a company can be critical. Low availability can cause holdups and standstills in production. You can address this problem by re-equiping your production. The more important the procurement object is for your production and the more difficult it is to re-equip your machines, however, the least attractive that option appears. Procurement is really in trouble, however, when there is not enough raw material for production (e.g. sheet metal).

Moreover, procurement is in an extremely difficult position in times of changes when sales figures are dropping and sales estimates have to be adjusted continuously. If a supplier has begun to rely on your periodic ordering system and has adjusted his materials planning accordingly, he might already have produced parts you might not need any more and are therefore not going to order. Due to his long-term materials scheduling he might have accumulated inventory levels for several years ahead. But who is going to pay for that? What will be paid by whom and when? Market conditions can result in a discrepancy between the quantities produced and the quantities needed. This can cause major disputes between suppliers and customers and may shake up the foundations on which a company is built. Innovative small and medium-sized businesses which have a high degree of flexibility but relatively limited financial assets are especially prone to be affected by that kind of problem.

(3) Price adjustments mean either higher or lower prices. As a cost factor, higher prices do not necessarily need to have bad consequences for your company. This depends on whether you are able to compensate for the increase in materials costs - without affecting your position in the market - by increasing your own sales prices. Another question is how unexpected and significant the price increase is and how limited your room for manoeuvre. Extreme price increases, i.e. price explosions, may force you to take a product out of your product range because you may no longer be able to sell it at a competitive price. Price decreases, on the other hand, are usually welcome, especially when they affect commodity prices world-wide. The first company to be in a position to use lower purchase prices for cost calculations can gain a considerable competitive edge, the more so as other companies might still carry considerable quantities of the respective product on stock. Economic principles would force these companies to devaluate their inventories at considerable cost.

Sales forces are usually very quick to take advantage of price decreases to boost their market share. This is not always clever though. Whether you can actually gain from such cost advantages or not depends on how fierce competition is in your market. The question is whether you want your procurement activities to be completely dependent on your sales activities and allow them to be more easily affected by price fluctuations. Is it viable to increase inventory levels when market prices are low? How do you know that prices have actually reached rock-bottom? Dealing in futures and options is one way of securing the supply of materials at a set or expected price.

4) Schedule adjustments are interesting from two points of view.

When procurement activities are synchronised with production and/or sales activities even the slightest adjustments in schedules can be significant. Early delivery can be as critical as late delivery. And it does not matter at all whether a delay has been caused by a strike, traffic jam or mistakes in placing the order. Early delivery, however, does not always have to be a disadvantage. In the plant-making business early delivery of tools and prototypes can actually be an advantage as certain processes can be carried out earlier than scheduled.

(5) Local adjustments can be important but do not usually cause major problems. Even if the political circumstances in a country result in the closure of a supply market, international companies are normally in a position to obtain procurement objects from other sources. Quality and performance levels may be affected, however. Another problem are mistakes which are made when selecting possible supply sources. The more subsupplier your supplier has, the higher the security of supply for your company in case of Force Majeure or unexpected increases in the required quantity of materials.

Illustration 17 shows what kind of problems are most likely to arise under what kind of circumstances.

Consequences of supply problems / Supply market problems	Performance adjustment	Quantity adjustment	Price adjustment	Schedule adjustment	Local adjustment
Supplier's reluctance to deliver	X	X		X	
Supplier's monopolistic behaviour	X	X	X	X	
Supplier's financial problems	X	X	X	X	
Supplier's bankrupcy		X		X	X
Supplier's quality problems	X				
Supplier's quantity problems		X		X	
Competitive disruptions in market		X	X	X	
Bottleneck in supply		X	X		
Oversupply		X	X		
Price explosion		X	X		

Illustration 17: Consequences of supply market problems

Illustration 18 illustrates how procurement problems and product characteristics correlate.

Decisive product criteria / Consequences	Singular product	Cheap product	Top product	Standard product	Established product	Innovative product	Customer-specific product	etc.
Performance adjustment	X		X			X	X	
Quantity adjustment	X	(X)	X			X	X	
Price adjustment		(X)			(X)		X	
Schedule adjustment	X	X	X	(X)	X	X	X	
Local adjustment	X	X	X	(X)	X	X	X	

Illustration 18: Correlation between procurement problems and product characteristics

4.12 Procurement Targets Define Courses of Action

Let us presume that targets, strategies and measures correlate as shown in Illustration 19.

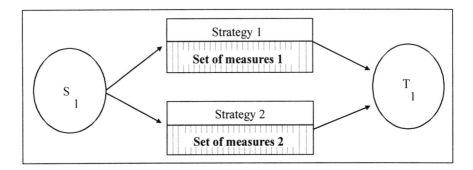

Illustration 19: The correlation between targets, strategies and measures in procurement

Based on a situation S1 a target T2 has to be achieved. Specific situations are defined by specific problems and potentials. There are several ways of reaching set targets. While Strategy No.1 may be a global sourcing approach, Strategy No.2 might focus on modular sourcing. The procurement strategy you choose determines your possible courses of action and therefore needs to be defined in detail. The selection and combination of adequate measures in procurement is what we call "procurement marketing mix". In order to avoid internal and external conflicts you need to establish a transparent target structure.

(1) Basic corporate targets

By setting basic targets we decide on a certain entrepreneurial attitude. These targets are of elementary significance for all corporate functions as they are the basis for all corporate activities. Basic corporate targets are set with a long-term view and cannot simply be changed overnight because they are used by different departments for deriving corresponding functional targets. Permanent changes risk upsetting corporate as well as functional overall plans. Instead of concentrating on the realization of targets too much time would be spent on adjusting and re-adjusting objectives. Illustration 20 shows possible combinations of basic targets (Meyer 1986, pp. 64).

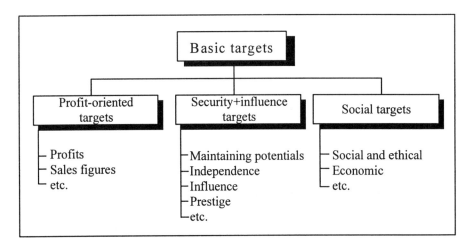

Illustration 20: A selection of basic targets in procurement

According to Illustration 20 the focus is clearly on profit-oriented targets, while socially-oriented targets are secondary. Under certain circumstances, e.g. in medium-sized family businesses, targets regarding security may be more important than others. It is important to define basic corporate targets first and then to identify secondary targets. From that set of overall targets functional targets can be derived.

(2) Basic procurement targets

Basic corporate targets are a guideline for a great number of functional targets. Defining targets, however, is not as important as knowing how to apply them in a decision-making process. A high level of abstraction when defining targets is essential for securing their subsequent intra- and interfunctional compatibility. Supply problems, e.g., have to be addressed and solved both internally and cross-functionally. If, for example, your company's products are more expensive than comparable products of your competitors, you have to work out in which corporate functions you may be able to reduce cost. You should also try to identify ways of increasing perfomance levels in procurement and other corporate functions in order to achieve an overall cost reduction in your company. You could, for example, seek to increase the quality of your sales operations and achieve an overproportional increase in your sales prices by marginally increasing sales costs.

The functional target structure shown in Illustration 21 is a starting point for comprehensive procurement strategies.

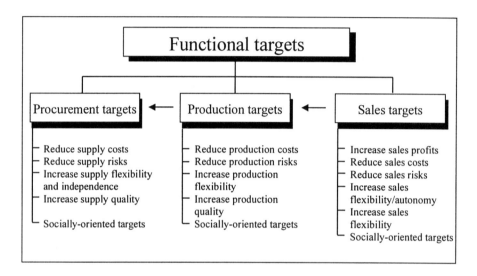

Illustration 21: Selection of functional targets

Reducing supply costs seems to be the most important issue nowadays. However, you should not only attempt to reduce the costs of the procurement object as such, i.e. unit prices, but also the procurement process costs which are generated by market research, need analysis, sourcing, supplier identification and negotiations, order processing, finance, stockkeeping and logistics, waste disposal and controlling.

There are different possibilities for increasing quality levels in procurement. The basic objective is to make sure that the services rendered actually meet corporate demands. This can lead to a higher continuity in overall performances as well as an increase in the quality of specific performances. The performances have a so-called object component (procurement tools, quantities) and a modality component (time and place of delivery, service, communication, terms of payment).

Supply risks indicate low availibility of performance and are tied to the quality of the performance rendered. Illustration 15 shows which factors mainly influence procurement risks.

Attempts to increase supply flexibility aim at increasing future rooms for manoeuvre. Performance flexibility too has an object component (procurement tools, quantities) and a modality component (time and place of delivery, service, communication, terms of payment terms). The more difficult sales forecasts in your line of business are, the more important flexibility is because you need to be able to adjust costs and performances to swiftly changing market conditions.

Socially-oriented procurement targets may also be of importance, for example when realizing special procurement projects abroad.

(3) Concrete procurement targets

After having defined general procurement targets, a set of concrete targets can be developed as shown in Illustration 22.

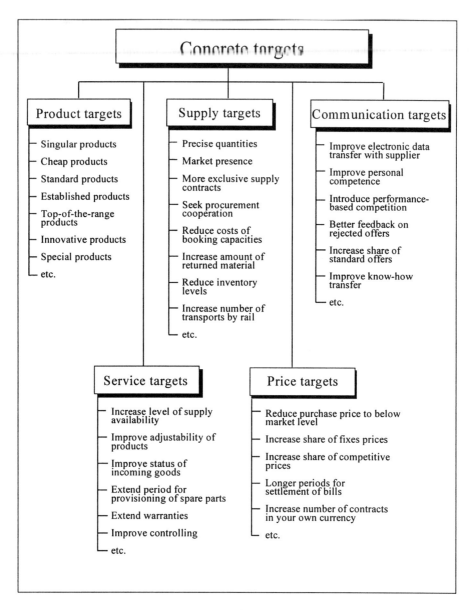

Illustration 22: Possible procurement targets

Purchasers can choose from a variety of procurement targets. When identifying several targets at the same time, however, it is essential to establish whether these targets are compatible in the first place.

(4) Procurement strategies

How can you achieve the targets you have set, and which procurement strategies should you apply?

Having defined strategies as a "set of suitable measures for achieving a certain target", we can categorize strategies either according to the targets set or the measures applied. Illustration 23 shows an empirical catalogue of possible measures in procurement.

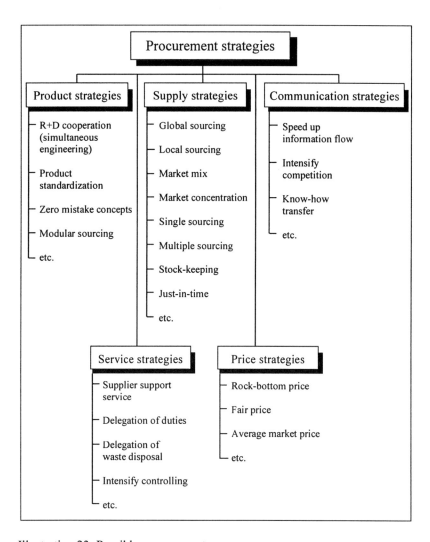

Illustration 23: Possible procurement measures

The strategies which are most commonly used in procurement are either context related or product related. As these strategies are widely known there is no need to explain them here. Instead, we will focus on working out how procurement targets and
comprehensive strategies interact. Illustration 24 shows which strategies might be best
suited for achieving specific targets in procurement.

Strategies / Targets		Costs	Performance	Flexibility	Risks
Product	R+D cooperation	X	X		
	Product standardization	X		X	X
	Zero mistake concept	X	X		X
	Modular sourcing	X	X		
Service	Supplier support service	X	X		X
	Performance service	X	X	X	
	Waste disposal service	X	X	X	X
	Intensify controlling		X		X
Supply	Global sourcing	X	X	X	
	Local sourcing				X
	Single sourcing	X	X		
	Multiple sourcing			X	X
	Market mix			X	X
	Market concentration	X	X		
	Stock-keeping				X
	Just-in-time	X		X	
Price	Rock-bottom price	X			
	Fair price		X	X	X
	Average market price			X	X
Communi-cation	Speed up information flow	X	X	X	X
	Intensify competition	X	X		
	Know-how-Transfer		X		

Illustration 24: Suitable strategies for achieving procurment targets

(5) Correlating targets in sales and procurement

Process-orientation in a company can help to prevent one-sided views in procurement.
Just look at the networking potentials. For example, some typical sales targets create
problems in materials planning and scheduling (see Illustration 25). If you want to

produce top products, however, you have to examine which main targets they have to fulfil. If you were responsible for purchasing parts for the Leica camera "L8", for example, you might have to buy standard products (material, screws etc), established products (reels etc), state-of-the-art products (lenses etc) and innovative products (closing lids etc). When classifying the targets which need to be fulfilled by a procurement object, the economic principle applies (realizing a certain target with the lowest possible input).

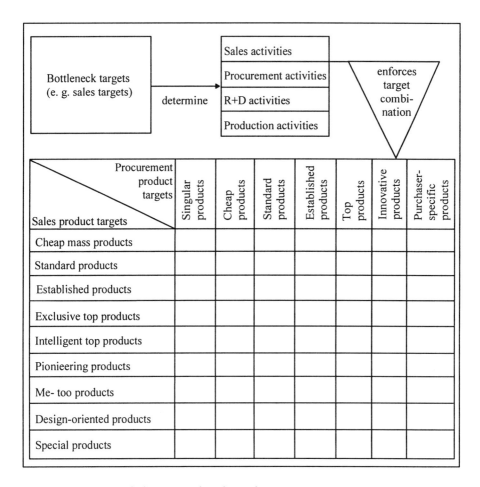

Illustration 25: Correlating targets in sales and procurement

4.13 Procurement Potentials Define the Room for Manoeuvre

One of the first decisions you have to make in procurement planning is whether you want to look for short-term or long-term potentials. Assuming that there are no short-term potentials in the first place may impede growth. When taking a long-term view, however, you have to decide which potentials you want to make use of, and how, and for whom, and at what cost.

Important information about the strenghts and weaknesses of a company can be obtained through an analysis of corporate potentials. According to Hammer this information can be used for strategical decisions (see Hammer 1982, p. 30). In 1981, Kreikebaum had already described the evaluation of corporate potentials as "an analysis of the resources of a company with a view to their importance for strategical decisions" (see Kreikebaum 1981, p.59).

Any evaluation of corporate and functional strengths and weaknesses is prone to be subjective. It is not so much having to list facts (e.g. staff numbers), but having to make assessments as well (staff qualification and motivation). For that kind of analysis you require a comprehensive set of tools. The question is whether to use an absolute set of tools ("Is the qualification of our staff up-to-date?") or to design a set of tools for comparing your company's performances with the ones of your competitors ("How good are our employees in comparison with our competitor's employees?").

Apart from having to conduct a need analysis of the present situation, you need to make sure you are using up-to-date information. Evaluations of corporate potentials conducted three years prior to your needing them will hardly be of use for today's decisions. Important employees may have left the company since then, or new employees might have joined in the meantime, thus increasing corporate potentials.

But how much into detail do you want to go when evaluating potentials? Do you want to analyse entire departments or just some of your employees? If you analyse individual employees, you will have to decide whether one highly qualified person with potential is more important to you than two members of staff who are less efficient and adaptable. And once you have singled out a particular employee and want him or her to deal with more demanding tasks, you will have to find another person to take over his or her daily business.

Finally, people have to be selected who are capable of using a specially designed set of tools for staff assessment. Hardly anybody would conduct such an evaluation without having a specific target in mind. A new head of department might assess staff performance as being "low" when starting his job, and later claim that any improvements in staff performances have been achieved due to his leadership. After two years he could say that he has managed to increase staff qualification and motivation through continuous training and encouragement. It is therefore important not to forget to evaluate first the potentials and motives of those people who will be entrusted with staff assessment projects. The process structure in Illustration 26 indicates a possible approach for analysing procurement potentials.

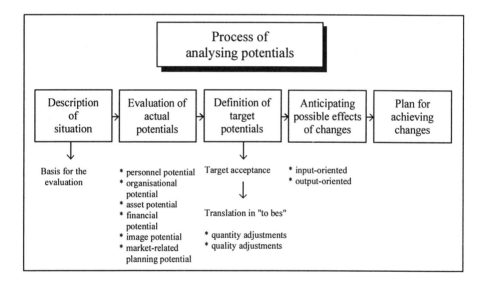

Illustration 26: A possible process for analysing procurement potentials

Based on the assumption that there are no absolute but only situation-oriented evaluations of corporate strengths and weaknesses it is necessary to define a suitable and targeted set of tools.

Several categories of corporate potentials need to be identified and evaluated. The category "staff potential" includes the variables staff numbers, staff qualification, staff motivation etc. The categories "staff potential" and "organisational potential" are closely connected. You can give a highly demanding job to qualified staff as long as you give them enough room for manoeuvre and allow them to use their skills independently. Or you let less qualified staff do the job because they are cheaper. Existing staff potential can be used more efficiently through projects and teamwork. The category "object potential" deals with the assessment of existing equipment (computers etc.), tools (databases etc.), and facilities (transport and storage facilities etc.). The category "financial potential" is very important as your financial assets have the power to either limit or increase your entrepreneurial room for manoeuvre. The "image potential" reflects the image of the buying company in the supply market. The position of a purchaser can be enhanced through his company's established products and favourable sales figures. If his company has a good reputation, he is more likely to be regarded as a reliable and trustworthy business partner and will be able to secure his supplier's cooperation even in difficult projects like value analyses. Finally, the procurement function should evaluate the market-oriented category "planning potential" on the sales side. Procurement costs increase automatically when sales planning is bad (cancellation charges, last minute orders). Unless the sales department has to take responsibility for such cost increases, they will never try to improve their overall planning.

"To be" potentials are potentials which result from basic corporate targets and are desirebale but have not been realized. "Zero Base" budgeting enables you to fix a new cost budget based on selected priorities. Let us presume that, in accordance with Gutenberg's law of balanced corporate planning (see Gutenberg 1983, pp. 163), a bottleneck in supply has been identified and a suitable set of measures agreed upon. Target-oriented "to bes" can be translated into adjustments in quality and quantity. Depending on the circumstances, adjustments can mean both increases or decreases.

A target-oriented derivation of "to bes" should always be accompanied by an assessment of the effects the corresponding adjustments might have. First of all, an input forecast has to be made: what would the adjustments cost? Moreover, an output analysis has to be made: how would the adjustments affect quality, quantity, flexibility, risk, and costs? This assessment will show you whether the planned adjustments are viable and profitable.

Depending on which "to be" potentials you want to realize, suitable steps have to be taken. If you want to increase your staff potential, for example, you may decide to employ new and better qualified people, you might schedule staff training, or you might even change your management style in order to increase staff motivation.

There are several ways of identifying and presenting potentials. The use of a polar profile for the presentation of data is particularly commendable. Illustration 27 shows how circumstances determine which potentials are important for a decision and which are not.

Conditions / Potentials	Singular product	Cheap product	Standard product	Established product	Top product	Innovative product	Purchaser-specific product	Quantity significance	etc.
Personnel potential	X	X	(X)	X	X	X	X	X	
Organisational potential	X					X	X	X	
Asset potential		X				X	X	X	
Financial potential					X		X	X	
Image potential	X						X	X	
Planning potential									

Illustration 27: Circumstances determine potentials

Working out a product-specific standard profile and comparing it with the actual profile can help to plan and initiate measures which suit a specific situation best. Illustration 28 shows a possible standard profile.

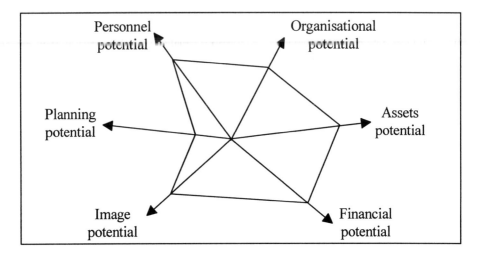

Illustration 28: Standard profile of a purchaser-specific product

Illustration 29 shows a possible profile in a concrete situation.

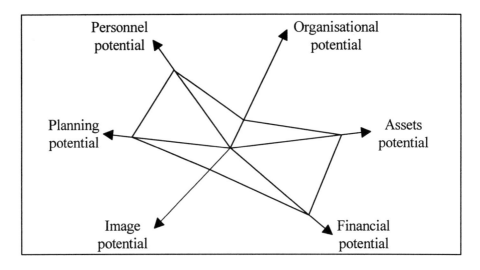

Illustration 29: Profile in a concrete demand situation

Both image potentials and organisational potentials are most vulnerable areas in a company. Improvements have to be encouraged strongly where necessary. When you realize in a certain situation that there is more potential than required, you can decide to use is later. This basic decision depends entirely on the situation and not so much on a specific procurement object. At that stage the decision-making process is very general whereas in the subsequent stages the purchaser has to focus on the details he needs when buying materials, semi-finished products or machines.

4.2 Need Analysis

Most procurement projects and activities start with an evaluation of the needs and requirements of a company. When other departments, e.g. construction or production, are entitled to and capable of placing outside orders themselves, the entire idea of maintaining separate purchasing departments is at stake. Where the purchasing function is being reduced to simply fulfilling objectives which have been set by construction, production or other corporate functions, however, there tend to be no processes for coordinating overall corporate targets.

Errors which occur in the stage of need analysis affect all subsequent procurement activities. When negotiating with suppliers not even the best incentive-contribution strategies can make up for initial mistakes in establishing corporate demands. It is therefore essential to look into this problem more closely. We will show how supply requirements influence the entire decision-making process.

4.21 Criteria for a Need Analysis

Before looking into the details of conducting a need analysis we have to decide whether such an analysis is necessary for every procurement object in the first place. Given that in most companies staff and time capacities are limited, the question is with which products to begin and how to use existing ressources most efficiently.

(1) The easiest solution would be to simply start with the purchasing object next on your list. That way you could gradually analyse all your procurement objects. The problem is, however, that important purchasing objects categorized, e.g., as "established procurement objects" might be analysed very late or not at all.

(2) The most commonly conducted analysis is probably the *ABC* analysis (see Illustration 30).

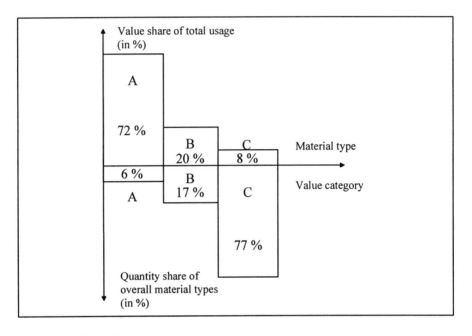

Illustration 30: ABC analysis

A product which sells well usually belongs to category *A* and therefore seems well worth a need analysis. This is only true, however, if the target of the analysis is to evaluate the product´s turnover in the first place. In other words, if the target is to increase the quality of a product´s performance, its turnover is hardly a suitable indicator. Illustration 31 indicates how this problem can be solved by re-naming the axes of an *ABC* analysis.

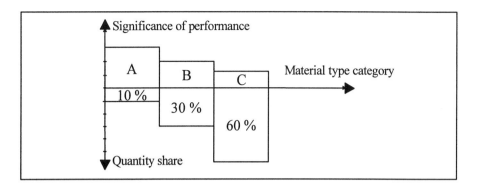

Illustration 31: Evaluation of materials based on performance priorities

Other targets, such as flexibility and risk, can be assessed corrspondingly.

(3) Another evaluation method is to combine a XYZ analysis with an ABC analysis as indicated in Illustration 32.

Value Exactness of forecasting	High usage value A	Medium usage value B	Low usage value C
High exactness of forecast X	high level of attention		
Medium exactness of forecast Y		medium level of attention	
Low exactness of forecast Z			low level of attention

Illustration 32: Combined XYZ and ABC analyses

Procurement objects categorized as XA, XB and YA are most suitable for a detailed need analysis.

56

(4) A performance-cost matrix can also be useful. In such a matrix two targets correlate (see Illustration 33). The performance aspects describe the output effect, i.e. the market effect, while the cost aspect focuses on the input or internal effects.

Costs \ Performance	high	low
high	1	2
low	3	4

Illustration 33: Performance/cost matrix

Our recommendation is to start with procurement objects categorized in class one and carry on with classes two, three and four in the indicated order. Similar matrixes can be worked out for other procurement targets.

(5) But what about less important procurement objects? If you want to concentrate on important procurement objects first in order to secure optimum conditions as quickly as possible you will have to leave the evaluation of less important products and services to a third party. This means the outsourcing of procurement objects which are not critical to your business. It seems even more attractive to outsource such responsibilities when you are implementing process orientation strategies in your company as the corresponding process costs are relatively stable. Whether you place small or large orders, the costs for each purchase are fixed. Many purchasing offices and agencies offer services which include the preparation, placement and monitoring of orders, especially for C-parts. The expert use of special information and processing methods and the coordination of orders have an enormous cost savings potential.

4.22 Supply Requirements

Before looking into the needs and requirements of a company more closely, let us address a few essential questions first. As shown in Illustration 34 the essential questions in procurement are what, when and how much.

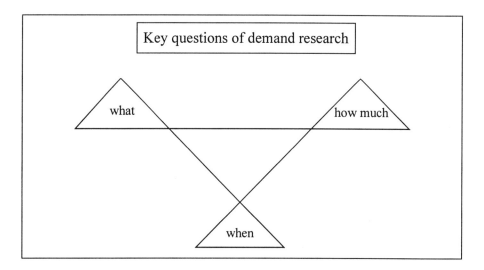

Illustration 34: The three essential questions in procurement

Furthermore, we have to ask the following questions:

- Is x really necessary?
- Why is x really necessary?
- Is "less" an option?
- Will the customer appreciate "more"?
- Is it possible and useful to standardize x?

It is hardly possible to make a list of every possible supply requirement a company may have. However, as later adjustments can be very costly, it is important to define as many supply requirements as possible prior to starting a need analysis. Special thought should be given to possibilities for networking purchasing efforts with other corporate functions. Illustration 35 shows some supply requirements which are essen-

58

tial criteria in decision-making processes.

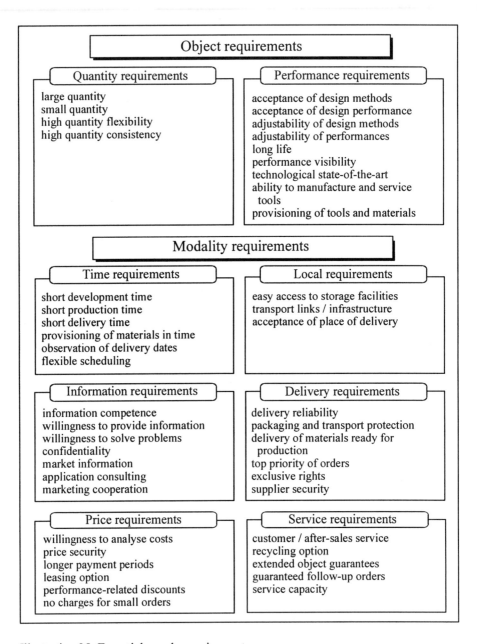

Illustration 35: Essential supply requirements

(1) The *performance requirements* to be fulfilled by a procurement object indicate which qualities the object needs to have. We could therefore call them quality requirements as well. Construction, R+D or the design departments may, for example, demand certain standards in construction and design. Drawings may include not only instructions regarding dimensions but also specify materials, colours, construction methods, special parts, etc. We can call this assessment criterion *design methods*.

In some situations you might decide that the construction department of a supplier is more competent and suitable for a project than your own. In such a case you can provide your supplier with information on the performances required by your company without actually supplying concrete solutions. This could be described as *design performance*. While the supply requirement *design methods* focuses on the input, *design performance* emphasizes the output.

Design solutions, however, do not last forever. The above mentioned requirements therefore have to be evaluated under the aspect of their adaptability to changes. The adaptability of design methods means that procurement objects are designed in a way which permits alterations in design methods, i.e. input. On the other hand, the adaptability of performances reflects the possibility to adjust performance outputs. We can call this supply requirement *performance flexibility*. As corporate sales departments will demand that products are adjusted to market requirements more swiftly in the future, this supply requirement will become increasingly important. This particularly applies to modular sourcing strategies.

Performance consistency is the supply requirement which indicates how long a procurement object can perform without any major decreases in performance levels.

Performance continuity, on the other hand, stands for utmost stability in quality levels, i.e. a procurement object needs to fulfill all defined requirements at all times. Fluctuations in quality are accepted only as long as they are within defined tolerances.

A special case of performances adaptability is when purchased parts can be used in more than one way and incorporated in different types of end products. This limits the range of products to be purchased as well as the processing costs in procurement.

Some procurement objects are incorporated into devices in a way that they can actually be seen by the final customer. In that case their design must indicate the quality and reliability of their performance. This supply requirement is called *performance visibility*.

It is not always possible to forecast exactly what a procurement object will look like and what kind of changes it might experience in the future. In order to be able to keep up with technological developments, it is essential to buy state-of-the-art objects. Suppliers should therefore work with the latest technical production methods and machines (CAD, CAM, etc.).

Another factor should also be considered: the possibility to machine and service special tools for production in-house. If a supplier is not capable of doing something himself, he might agree to the purchasing company providing the materials and tools which meet the required standards (*provisioning of tools and materials*).

(2) *Quantity requirements* seem obvious enough not to have to be explained here.

(3) *Time requirements* can be significant. Short development times can offer major advantages, especially when you are planning to launch new products. One of your suppliers may be able to develop a new product or part quicker than his competitors. Furthermore, production lead times are of importance because your supplier needs to be able to produce a procurement project within the time required. Delivery time is another well-known criterion: has your supplier taken appropriate steps to secure short delivery times by increasing emergency stock levels or by using faster means of transport? If you prefer delivery on a fixed date to delivery within a certain delivery time, your supplier needs to be able to meet your delivery deadlines, be it ex works or free delivery. This is the more important for industrial organisations which have implemented JIT. In trading organisations delivery dates are usually fixed.

You may prefer more flexible materials scheduling, however, and ask your supplier to adjust his materials scheduling accordingly.

(4) *Local requirements* are obvious and do not need to be explained here.

(5) *Information requirements*: The more popular outsourcing is becoming with com-

panies, the more information is growing in importance in procurement.

Requiring a high level of *information competence* from your supplier means that you want your supplier to know more about something than you do. If you want to take advantages of your supplier´s specialist know-how, you have to make sure that he has such know-how in the first place.

But the mere knowledge that your supplier does have some useful know-how is not enough. He also has to be willing to exchange information and share his know-how with you. This applies to companies as a whole as much as to the people acting on be-half of their companies. If your counterparts refuse to part with essential information, your supplier´ s competence will hardly be of use to you. On the other hand, informa-tion flow and shared competence can result in a comprehensive know-how transfer. Sharing specialist or even confidential information can help to reduce time and costs in procurement.

If you secure your supplier´s *willingness to exchange information* with you, he may eventually be prepared to work with you on identifying possible supply solutions. Cross-company team work and project management can support mutual cooperation efficiently.

The willingness to look for possible solutions together can be limited by the desire to keep certain information confidential. This desire can be as much on your part as on your supplier´s. Utmost confidentiality is imperative when your supplier provides you with confidential information, e.g. on developments and procedures, or you supply him with classified information. This might mean that entire projects might have to be developed strictly confidentially. However, this is easier said than done.

Apart from the above mentioned essential supply requirements your company might need more specific information. Up-to-date, comprehensive market information is a viable tool for sourcing activities. If you discover price and quantity problems in the market early, you may be able to take appropriate steps in time. If you observe new trends in products and processes in the market, you might be able to give important input to your construction and design departments. When new products, systems or technical equipment are introduced in your company, your staff needs to be trained ac-cordingly. You can ask your supplier to provide the necessary information and consulting services.

Moreover, when a new product has been launched, your sales department may ask your suppliers to do some marketing for your company in order to promote your innovation more widely. This supply requirement is called *marketing cooperation.*

(6) Another important supply requirement are your *delivery requirements. Delivery reliability* means that your supplier can fulfill all instructions regarding performance levels, quantities, delivery dates and delivery places within the stipulated time. You can rely on him.

There can be more specific demands regarding the delivery of goods as well, however. You may require particularly high quality of packaging and transport if delicate or hazardous procurement objects have to be handled.

Delivering materials in a way that it is ready for production can reduce costs and time for handling, for example, the unwrapping or repacking of materials.

Asking your supplier to give your orders top priority tends to be necessary in bottleneck situations or when you order procurement objects for an early stage of production from a new supplier or a single source.

If a procurement object is of major significance for the competitive value of a product, you might want to secure some *exclusive rights.* Exclusive contracts can give you a competitive edge, even though you might not be able to gain from time and market related price reductions. This becomes even more of an issue when you integrate your suppliers more closely in product development processes. The car industry has been doing this very successfully in recent years.

Another important supply requirement is the *financial soundness and stability of your supplier.* Your supplier needs to be financially sound and technically well equipped. He should not be too dependant on his subsuppliers and seek for cooperation and partnership in long-term business relationships.

(7) From the purchaser's point of view the *price requirements* are always of utmost importance.

It goes without saying that we would all prefer to get our procurement objects free of charge or, at least, a lot cheaper than our competitors. But this is hardly realistic.

Conducting a cost analysis together with your supplier is a much more helpful and realistic approach for identifying potentials for cost reductions. After having set a target price, a systematical analysis is conducted to find out which purchase costs are going to incurr. This kind of analysis can only be realized through long and open conversations with your supplier and might require that your supplier allows you to see his calculations. This kind of open communication might also lead to new ways of production. Partnership and cooperation are the prerequisites for the *willingness to conduct mutual cost analyses*. If you only want to see your supplier's calculations to be able to demand price reductions later, however, he is not very likely to trust you ever again. The same applies when you do not order the big volumes you had misleadingly promised your supplier. If you place a much smaller order, your supplier will struggle to deliver at the low price he had calculated for a much bigger order volume. The lack of any strategic thinking in this field is the reason why not many purchasers really gain from conducting cost analyses with their suppliers.

Price fluctuations in the field of commodities, i.e. standard products, are difficult to anticipate. In certain lines of business, e.g. in plant making and in the production of some consumer goods, sales profits tend to be relatively fixed. It may be advisable to fix accepted margins for fluctuations here. This means, however, that you may not always be able to get rock-bottom prices. Cost price fluctuations, on the other hand, can be caused by currency fluctuations. You can gain from the devaluation of a currency, for example the Italian lira, if you have concluded your purchase contract in this currency. When you do business with Japan and the value of the Yen starts soaring, however, you might lose money. If you want to avoid the risk of currency fluctuations and are willing to forego any possible advantages, you are well advised to conclude your contracts in your own currency only. This supply requirement is called *price security*.

A company with limited financial means can ask for payment terms which allow for late settlement. Such a company might also be interested in leasing machines and equipment to tie up a minimum of capital while at the same time securing state-of-the-art in their production. Leasing can also be a solution for increasing flexibility in quantities, especially when orders are placed at short notice.

64

Especially in trade, companies try to negotiate big discounts for special quantities or performances. Discounts are even more often requested for no other purpose but to demonstrate and exert purchasing power. In business relationships which are based on cooperation and partnership you should only demand performance-related discounts. Many industrial enterprises, however, are happy enough if they do not to have to pay additional charges when ordering small quantities.

(8) Last but not least we should look into the supply requirement *service requirements*: The value of the procurement object can be increased by additional services. Services can include installation and set-up, repairs and maintenance (i.e. customer services). Moreover, they can include deinstallation and recycling as well as guarantees and warrantees.

In addition to offering special services for a procurement object, more general services can be provided. You may use your supplier's facilities and capacities for testing, development, inventories etc. We call this supply requirement *service capacity*.

When faced with a specific entrepreneurial decision you should check which supply requirements are most important for your company and discuss these supply requirements with other corporate functions. In such discussions you might learn about potential problems in the future and you will therefore need to specify the supply requirements listed above in more detail. In a previous publication (see Koppelmann 1995, pp 147) a checklist for such discussions has been developed. Only close cooperation with all corporate functions will ensure that real requirements are identified in a supply situation.

4.23 Supply Requirement Priorities

After having established which general supply requirements a company might have, we want to use so-called "if-conditions" (see chapter 3.3) to evaluate which supply requirements are important in which situation. Illustration 38 demonstrates how your requirements may, for example, depend on whether you want to buy top or standard products.

The index indicates the importance of different requirements, with x_1 meaning very important, x_2 important, and x_3 not so important.

This matrix can be used as a systematic control tool which supports the coordination process with other corporate functions. It provides the basis for rational decisions. Deviations are only allowed under special circumstances. This kind of transparent decision-making tool makes it easier for incoming team members to take over their new responsibilities.

Conditions (Object characteristics) → / ↓ Supply requirements		Singular product	Cheap product	Standard product	Established product	Top product	Innovative product	Purchaser-specific product	Significance of quantity	etc.
Quantity requirements	large quantity		X_1	X_1	X_2				X_1	
	small quantity	X_1					X_2	X_2	X_2	
	high significance of quantity				X_2				X_2	
	high quantity consistency					X_1	X_1	X_1	X_1	X_1
Performance requirements	acceptance of design methods	X_1				X_1	X_1	X_1		
	acceptance of design performances	X_1				X_1	X_1	X_1		
	adjustability of design methods						X_2			
	adjustability of performances					X_1	X_1	X_1	X_2	
	long life	X_2				X_1	X_2	X_2		
	performance consistency				X_1	X_1			X_1	
	application flexibility		X_2	X_1						
	visibility of performance					X_1	X_1			
	technological state-of-the-art	X_1				X_1	X_1	X_1		
	ability to manufacture tools	X_2					X_2	X_2		
	provisioning of tools and materials					X_2			X_3	
Schedule requirements	short development time					X_2	X_1	X_1		
	short production time		X_1		X_2				X_1	
	short delivery time		X_1		X_2				X_1	
	provisioning of materials in time				X_1	X_1			X_1	
	observation of delivery data	X_2	X_1	X_1	X_1				X_1	
	flexible scheduling				X_2	X_2				
location requirements	easy access to storage facilities		X_3		X_2				X_2	
	transport links / infrastructure		X_2		X_2				X_2	
	acceptance of place of delivery			X_2	X_2	X_2			X_2	
Delivery requirements	supplier reliability		X_1	X_2	X_1	X_1	X_1	X_1	X_1	
	packaging and transport protection	X_2				X_2	X_2	X_2		
	deliver materials ready for production		X_1	X_1	X_2				X_1	
	top priority of orders					X_2	X_2	X_1		
	exclusive rights					X_2	X_2	X_1		
	supplier security	X_1				X_1	X_1	X_1	X_1	
Price requirements	willingness to analyse costs	X_1				X_1	X_2	X_2	X_1	
	price security	X_2				X_2			X_2	
	longer payment periods	X_2						X_3		
	leasing option	X_2								
	performance-related discount					X_2			X_2	
	no charges for small orders				X_2	X_2				
Service requirements	after-sales-service	X_1				X_1	X_1	X_1		
	recycling option	X_2	X_1	X_2	X_2	X_2	X_2	X_2	X_1	
	extended object guarantee	X_1			X_2					
	guaranteed follow-up orders				X_1					
	service capacity	X_3				X_3	X_3	X_3		
Information requirements	information competence	X_2				X_1	X_1	X_1		
	willingness to provide information	X_2				X_1	X_1	X_1		
	willingness to solve problems	X_1				X_1	X_1	X_1		
	confidentiality					X_2	X_2	X_1		
	market information					X_2	X_2	X_2		
	application consulting	X_2				X_2	X_2	X_2		
	marketing cooperation					X_2	X_2			

Illustration 36: Situation-related requirement priorites

4.24 Need Analysis Methods

Need analysis means much more than just analysing required quantities.

(1) Performance analysis

An important part of any performance analysis is to conduct a value analysis with the target to create and increase value. Increases in value mean that the same or higher performances are achieved with less effort. Value analyses normally concentrate on technical aspects.

Sophisticated techniques are used to increase the room for manoeuvre in product design. Brainstorming in different corporate functions can help to identify new and innovative design solutions.

(2) Quantity analysis

Illustration 37 gives a comprehensive overview of established methods used for quantity analyses.

68

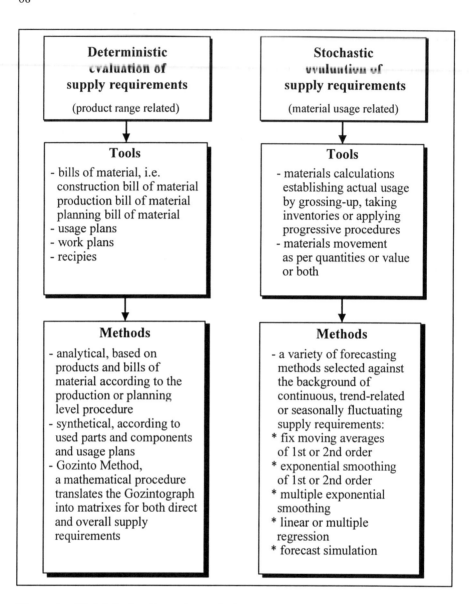

Illustration 37: Methods of quantity analysis

(3) Schedule analysis

If you are prepared to negotiate a long-term framework agreement with your supplier, you will have to secure the continuity of his production planning (see Illustration 38).

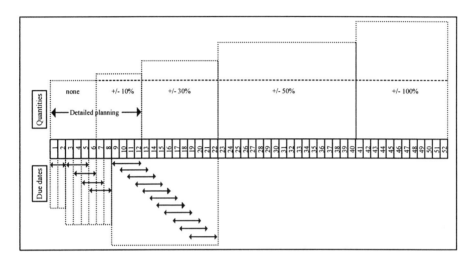

Illustration 38: Continuous Order Method

Let us assume you make a framework agreement for a duration of twelve months and agree that after every quarter it is prolonged automatically for another three months. In that particular case no changes in quantities are possible within the first six weeks. However, the quantities can be called off a week earlier or a week later than planned. Between week 7 and week 12 a quantity adjustment of +/- 10% is possible. Moreover, a time adjustment of three weeks is possible between week 3 and 8. Then, between week 13 and 22, quantity adjustments of +/- 30% are possible and time adjustments of up to four weeks between week 9 and 22. By this time at the latest the purchasing function must have been given the go ahead for buying materials for production as well as pre-fabricating. Between weeks 23 and 40 quantity adjustments of +/- 50% are allowed, and of as much as 100% between week 41 and 52.

(4) Price/Cost analysis

In most companies the times of progressive price calculations when costs and profits were added up to define the price of a product are long gone. Today, calculations are done by setting target prices which are deemed competitive. These prices determine the maximum cost of each object and process in a project. This approach is most helpful for making "make or buy" decisions. The question whether to purchase or produce parts will become even more imperative in the future.

4.25 Procurement or Production?

Once you know which goods and services you need, you have to address the question whether you should produce the respective part, component or service yourself or buy it from an outside source. Outsourcing is an option that should always be considered.

(1) Make or buy

Having to decide whether to make or buy a product is nothing new. Illustration 39 should therefore suffice to provide an overview of possible criteria for the decision-making process.

	Reasons for Make decision	Reasons for Buy decision
Quality	* close cooperation between construction and production when improving existing and developing new products * continous quality control * protecting corporate patents and know-how * acquiring specific production know-how	* targeted problem solutions possible due to specialization in R + D * high quality through specialization of means of production and facilities * comprehensive testing methods even for small batches * use of external patents
Capacities	* using existing capacities fully - personnel - means of production / facilities	* reduction of capacity bottlenecks, thus optimizing one's own production * specialized facilities are used fully and not left idle
Investments	* reducing taxable profits through investments * facilities potentials	* no capital is tied-up through special investments * important in-house parts
Costs	* no costs caused through - supplier profits - external transport and packaging costs * no costs arising from unjustified price increases on part of supplier (more independence from single sources)	* low unit prices due to specialization and high rate of capacity utilization * low unit prices due to site-related advantages - low-wage countries - subsidies - no environmental regulations * outsourcing of parts which do not contribute to corporate success * low R + D costs * low share of fixed costs * low inventory costs
Schedules	* quick response time in case of product type adjustments - innovations - fluctuations in production due to shorter ways of information and organisation as well as competence to issue direct instructions - no transport time required - direct control over production schedules	* short development time and shorter production lead times due to specialization * delivery on call on demand * getting rid of schedule bottlenecks in one's own production
Risk	* existing know-how does not leak to competitors * advanced integration of suppliers impeded * new developments are kept secret	* diversion of risk by working with several suppliers * low risks when production slows down or new developments have not been successfull * no risks caused by buying the wrong production material * no risks of scrap or waste material
Other's	* no suitable suppliers in the market * more independence of company due to increased depth of production * transport problems	* countertrade * complaints are impossible * small batches can be bought * one's own company can concentrade on core compentence parts

Illustration 39: Criteria for "Make or Buy" decisions

(2) Outsourcing

Outsourcing means that a decision has been made to change things. There are two ways of satisfying corporate demands through outsourcing: you can either let suppliers take over tasks which used to be the responsibility of one of your corporate functions, e.g. parts of the actual production. Or you can outsource corporate potentials and functions, e.g. production potentials.

In order to establish which party might be able to achieve the desired improvements it is necessary to check the costs and performances of all parties involved in the product development process. Improvements may mean cost reductions, increases in performance levels (quality) or higher flexibility (adaptability). When examining these factors you ought to concentrate on what some parties, including you, can do better than others. For identifying core competences, the following questions have to be addressed:

- What can you do better than others?
- What can others do better than you?
- Is there another way to improve your performances than letting others take over?
- Would your competence be affected by outsourcing?
- Will your company´s competitive position be affected by outsourcing parts of your corporate competence?
- Would it be possible to reverse the outsourcing project and produce in-house again?
- Would it make sense to agree on long-term contracts to limit the competence "drain"?
- Would you run the risk of confidential information and know-how being related to your competitors?

Other corporate functions also might prove to be "better suited" for a project than any outside parties. Do not forget that outsourcing can indeed cause major problems:

- *The job problem*: when corporate functions are outsourced it is not always guaranteed that the affected employees will be given new tasks in the company.
- *The decision making problem*: when functions and potentials are outsourced, the question whether to make or to buy parts becomes less important.
- *The management and control problem*: external management and control are much

more difficult than internal management.

– *The choice problem*: outsourcing can increase the number of alternatives to choose from.

– *The synergy problem*: existing networks are disrupted. The elimination of individual network modules can have consequences for other modules as well.

4.3 Evaluating and Selecting Supply Markets

In which markets shall we look for new suppliers? Which targets can we achieve in which markets? Is global sourcing really the ultimate solution? Special criteria for comparison and assessment are required for evaluating markets.

4.31 Market Characteristics

When looking into older publications about market mechanisms and their main characteristics (see Theism, 1970; Kraljic, 1977) you will find that a major focus used to be on the competition aspect. Some simpler models use the number of competitors in a market as a criterion for differenciation. Later Kraljic developed a more sophisticated model in which the supply market is defined by the evaluated suppliers, on the one hand, and the position of the buying company, on the other.

Markets can be assessed according to the characteristics performance, cost, and risk.

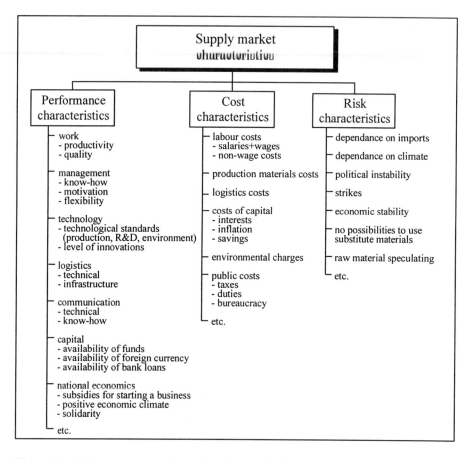

Illustration 40: Important supply market characteristics

The focus of the purchaser should be on evaluating performance levels. Other criteria, like costs and risks, should be secondary. These criteria are well known and do not require detailed explanations. When evaluating them, however, you should seek to analyse existing situations as well as potential future situations, thus securing a dynamic analysis.

4.32 Market Portfolio

For a start, let us have another look at the product-market matrix (see Illustration 41).

potential suppliers markets / procurement objects	old, established suppliers/markets	related suppliers/markets	new suppliers/markets
old procurement objects	purely repetitive purchases consolidating relationships	modified repetitive purchases extending the supply market	supply market variation
modified procurement objects	modified repetitive purchases buying new objects in established markets	modification in procurement (or variation)	supply market variation for modified procurement objects
new procurement objects	buying new objects in established markets (pure procurement variation)	procurement variation under consideration of related suppliers	procurement innovation

Illustration 41: Product-market matrix

While the placement of repetitive orders is standard procedure and therefore placed in the upper left corner of the matrix, procurement innovations are located in the bottom right corner. When launching a global sourcing project you would be ill advised to start with product innovations, as you would have to deal with the two risk factors "new market" and "new procurement object". The field of "supply market variation" seems much more suitable when engaging in global sourcing projects.

The illustrated assessment of supply markets can be refined by rating object characteristics as "more" or "less" important. As market evaluations are only interesting when conducted with a view to a concrete procurement object, we can use the decision-making criteria described before. If we regard market characteristics as market requirements, we can assess these requirements according to their importance, x_1 indicating great importance, x_2 medium importance, and x_3 low importance.

Conditions (object characteristics) / external market requirements		singular product	cheap product	standard product	established product	top product	innovative product	purchaser-specific product	significance of quantity	etc.
Performance	work performance	X_1			X_2	X_1	X_1	X_1	X_2	
	management performance	X_1				X_1	X_1	X_1	X_2	
	technology	X_1				X_1	X_1	X_1		
	logistics performance		X_1	X_1					X_1	
	communication performance	X_1				X_1	X_1	X_1		
	capital performance		X_2	X_2					X_2	
	national economics		X_2	X_2		X_3	X_3			
Cost	labour costs	X_2	X_1	X_1	X_1	X_2	X_2	X_2	X_1	
	material costs	X_2	X_1	X_1	X_1	X_2	X_2	X_2	X_1	
	logistics costs		X_1	X_1	X_1				X_1	
	cost of capital		X_2	X_2	X_2				X_2	
	environmental charges		X_2	X_2	X_2	X_3	X_2	X_2	X_2	
	taxes and duties	X_2	X_2	X_2	X_2	X_3	X_2	X_2	X_2	
Risik	dependance on imports		X_2		X_2				X_2	
	dependance on climate		X_1	X_1	X_1				X_1	
	political instability		X_2		X_1	X_2	X_2	X_2	X_1	
	strikes	X_1	X_2		X_1	X_1	X_1	X_1	X_1	
	economic instability	X_1	X_2		X_1	X_1	X_1	X_1	X_1	
	no possibility to use substitute material					X_2	X_2	X_2		
	raw material speculations				X_2	X_2			X_2	

Illustration 42: Object characteristics and market requirements

The position each object should have in a market can be derived from the matrix. When looking for a specific object (e.g. top product) it is necessary to find the markets which are characterized by the required position (see Illustration 43)

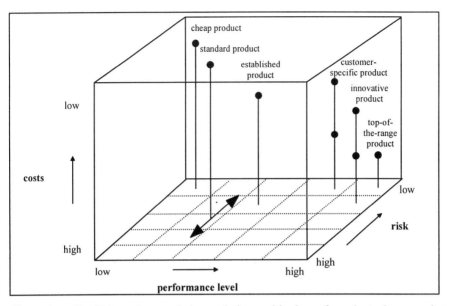

Illustration 43: Object characteristics and the positioning of products in a market

In Illustration 44 this model is refined by including the competition aspect mentioned before.

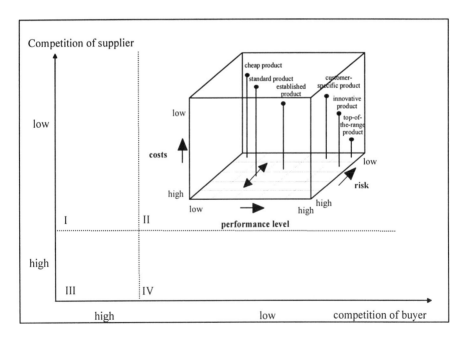

Illustration 44: Competition and the positioning of products in a market

4.33   Global Sourcing

Everybody is talking about global sourcing. But you have to analyse carefully whether such a strategy makes sense for your company or not. To secure corporate success, there has to be an overall concept of global selling, global production and global sourcing. Let us look at a company which has production facilities in one country, and exports world-wide. When this company decides to start buying materials and commodities in international markets, this alone does not make a global sourcing concept. In an international group, however, global sourcing activities can be handled by best practice functions in a centralized or decentralized way. Under these circumstances global sourcing tends to lead to single sourcing. Looking for best suppliers on world markets offers a number of possibilities:

- *Price potentials*: companies can reduce costs. Depending on input and realization costs some countries might offer more favourable net barter terms of trade or commodity terms of trade than others. This calls for a thorough evaluation. The multinational corporation IBM, for example, uses such evaluations as a basis for their "Make or Buy" decisions when developing new personal computers.

- *Performance potentials*: companies can benefit from the innovations and technological leadership of companies in other markets.

- *Flexibility potentials*: companies can benefit from increased capacities due to expanding markets. The more difficult it is to anticipate in-house demands exactly, the more critical are quantities and performance levels. Contracting suppliers who operate world-wide can help to outbalance fluctuations in demand.

Although there are considerable potentials in global sourcing, there are significant problems as well. For one, staff might be lacking the necessary skills. This obstacle, however, can be surmounted by targeted language training and lectures on the culture and customs of other nations. It is much more difficult, however, to overcome old prejudices and make purchasers believe in global sourcing strategies.

Furthermore, when going international there are considerable risks involved. The geographical distances increase the risk factor "delivery time". Even though a consignment has been shipped on schedule, logistical problems might cause delays in delivery. The distance can also increase the risk factors "quality" and "quantity". Any errors that might occur can cause delays and take up considerable management time. Currency fluctuations are another major risk when buying abroad. And do not forget to evaluate potential cost risks in the countries you decide to operate in: how will wages, energy prices and interest rates develop in the future? Distance also increases control risks. When buying in-house or from a supplier in your region, it is relatively easy and quick to solve supply problems. In global sourcing, however, problems have to be addressed in a much more formal way, with processes being prone to disruptions. Projects are much more complex, planning more difficult, preparation times longer, mistakes in planning more significant, and adjustments much slower.

When making a supply decision the criteria costs, performance levels and risks have to be assessed. When evaluating cost criteria, bear in mind to analyse the process costs as much as the unit prices of a procurement object. To make global sourcing a viable solution these costs have to be lower than they would be when buying in your own market, as much today as tomorrow. Future performances are also critical when looking into criteria like state-of-the-art, continuity and reliability. Political risks, currency fluctuations and environmental problems, however, are much more difficult to anticipate.

Obstacles can be surmounted by using the right methods and tools. Offering staff the opportunity to learn foreign languages and being introduced into different cultures is an excellent tool to improve staff attitude towards global sourcing. Sending out staff to work abroad for a while can be a valuable incentive, and many companies even regard such a work experience abroad as a prerequisite for a successful professional career. Gathering detailed information on markets is vital for decision-making processes. We will look into suitable methods of market evaluation in chapter 4.71. Especially smaller companies might find that the cooperation with other companies which share similar interests is a valuable sourcing solution. Procurement cooperation can be established which can result in an efficient sharing of tasks, splitting of markets, and allocation of responsibilities. That way one company could buy object A for all parties involved while another object B could be the responsibility of another company. Thus synergies are used and purchasing power is increased.

4.4 Supplier Evaluation

After having decided in which markets to look for suppliers, you have to define procedures for the evaluation and pre-selection of suppliers. The structure shown in Illustration 45 has proved to be quite helpful in the process.

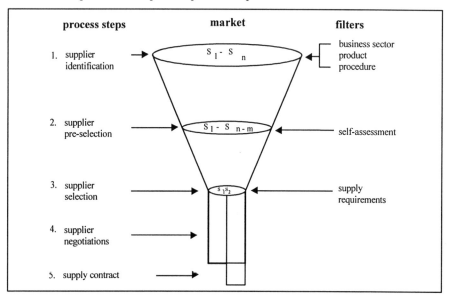

Illustration 45: Funnel model for supplier selection

4.41 Supplier Identification

Who supplies what? What is the best way to approach this question? The easiest way
is to start looking for product suppliers. The disadvantage of this very simple approach
is that it tends to focus on past performances and products. A manufacturer who produces water pumps of top quality might be capable of doing other things as well, but
nobody has asked for other performances yet or the manufacturer himself has not ad-
vertised his potentials effectively.

It can therefore be useful to take into consideration other lines of business as well
when looking for potential suppliers of a product. You could, e.g., consider manufac-
turers of all types of pumps. Then you might identify one or two suppliers who are in-

terested in extending their range of products. Such a supplier will be interested in supplying you with a new pump which is up to your standard. But this approach is not new.

A new approach when buying a purchaser-specific product, however, is to look for similarities with existing products and then look for suitable suppliers. For one, the similarity can be in the product. Or, products can be alike in the way they have been manufactured. In that case we would be looking for a supplier with special manufacturing skills, e.g., a manufacturer who can supply large quantities of special cast parts with high performance consistency. That means that we are defining some essential object requirements. Limiting the number of requirements helps to focus on the target of identifying potential suppliers in general. These object-specific requirements are important for the following pre-selection.

4.42 Supplier Pre-selection

Before taking a closer look at a selected number of suppliers, you should ask your potential suppliers to fill in a suitable self-assessment questionnaire. Illustration 46 shows some questions which could be used in such a questionnaire.

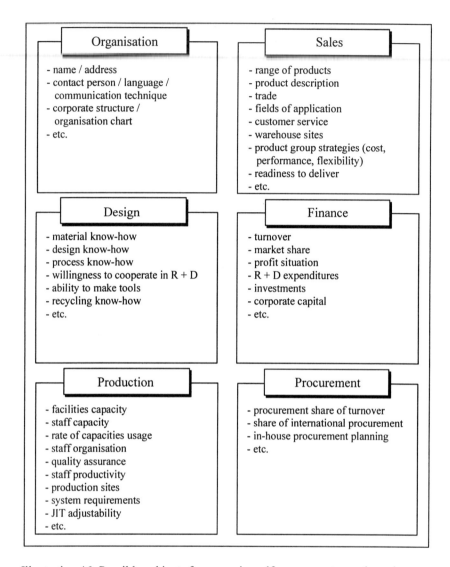

Illustration 46: Possible subjects for a suppier self-assessmant questionnaire

You can send a detailed questionnaire to a number of suitable supplicrs (S_1 - S_n) and ask them to fill them in and return them within a stipulated time. The actual response time, completeness and precision of your supplier's reply can already be regarded as an indicator for the way he deals with potential customers. When a supplier provides a jumble of additional information or leaves questions unanswered you can deduct how professional or interested he is in establishing a business relationship with you. These are only very general indicators, however. The problem is how to pre-select suitable suppliers and how to approach them. A well-known procedure is to decide under what kind of circumstances (if-component) the answers of a potential supplier (then-components) are crucial for the decision to be made. And in which case would a supplier's insufficient response or complete failure to answer your question result in the disqualification of that supplier?

Illustration 47 can help to find an approach to these questions.

supplier characteristics	procurement object characteristics	singular product	cheap product	standard product	established product	top product	innovative product	purchaser specific product	significance of quantity	etc.
Sales	range of products	X	X	X	X	X	X	X	X	
	product descriptions	X	X	X	X	X	X	X	X	
	trade			X						
	fields of application	X	X		X	X	X	X	X	
	customer service	X			X	X	X	X		
	warehouse site		X		X	X	X	X	X	
	cost reduction strategies		X						X	
	increase performance strategies	X			X	X	X	X		
	increase flexibility strategies				X	X	X	X	X	
	readiness to deliver		X		X	X	X	X	X	
Production	facilities capacity		X		X	X	X	X	X	
	staff capacity				X	X	X			
	capacity usage rate	X	X		X	X	X	X	X	
	quality assurance	X	X		X	X	X	X	X	
	staff organisation				X	X	X	X		
	staff productivity		X		X	X	X	X	X	
	production sites								X	
	system adjustability	X	X		X	X	X	X	X	
	JIT-adjustability		X	X	X	X	X	X	X	
Design	material know-how	X	X		X	X	X	X	X	
	design know-how	X	X		X	X	X	X	X	
	process know-how	X	X		X	X	X	X	X	
	cooperation in R+D					X	X	X		
	willingness to analyse		X		X	X	X	X	X	
	ability to make tools				X	X	X	X	X	
	recycling know-how		X	X	X	X	X	X	X	
Finance	turnover	X	X		X	X	X	X	X	
	market share	X	X		X	X	X	X	X	
	profit situation	X	X		X	X	X	X	X	
	R+D expenditure					X	X	X		
	investments					X	X	X	X	
	corporate capital	X	X		X	X	X	X	X	
Procurement	procurement share of turnover		X		X	X	X	X	X	
	international proc./total proc.		X		X				X	
	in-house procurement planning	X	X		X	X	X	X	X	

Illustration 47: Supplier pre-selection based on self-assessment questionnaires

In Illustration 47 we have marked all criteria in which your supplier's failure to provide the required information would prompt his disqualification.

4.43 Supplier Selection

All aspects mentioned above have to be taken into consideration when finally selecting your suppliers. Illustration 48 indicates the basic structure for defining supplier requirements.

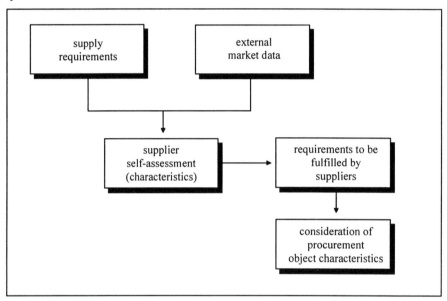

Illustration 48: How to define supplier requirements

The focus is on the requirements stipulated in Illustration 35. They are the basis for deciding whether it is worth at all to meet personally with a pre-selected supplier. Depending on the importance of the respective criteria, this could mean that in a certain supply situation (you need, e.g., top products) a supplier has to meet a least all x_1 requirements. Should he be unable to fulfill even these minimum requirements, this would be a reason for disqualifying him.

In Illustration 49 we have defined supply requirements as criteria to be fulfilled by a supplier and have put them in relation to requirement conditions, i.e. procurement object characteristics. The table illustrates which criteria are important for which objects.

Supplier selection criteria		Conditions (object characteristics)	Singular product	Cheap product	Standard product	established product	top product	innovative product	purchaser-specific product	significance of quantity	etc.
Quantity requirements		large quantity		X_1	X_1	X_2				X_1	
		small quantity	X_1				X_2	X_2	X_2		
		high significance of quantity			X_2					X_2	
		high quantity consistency				X_1	X_1	X_1	X_1	X_1	
Performance requirements		acceptance of design methods	X_1			X_1	X_1	X_1	X_1		
		acceptance of design performances	X_1			X_1	X_1	X_1	X_1		
		adjustability of design methods							X_2		
		adjustability of performances				X_1	X_1	X_1	X_1	X_2	
		long life	X_2			X_1	X_2	X_2			
		performance consistency			X_1	X_1				X_1	
		application flexibility		X_2	X_1						
		visibility of performance					X_1	X_1			
		technological state-of-the-art	X_1				X_1	X_1	X_1		
		ability to manufacture tools	X_2					X_2	X_2		
		provisioning of tools and materials				X_2				X_3	
Schedule requirements		short development time					X_2	X_1	X_1		
		short production time		X_1		X_2				X_1	
		short delivery time		X_1	X_1	X_2				X_1	
		provisioning of materials in time			X_1	X_1				X_1	
		observation of delivery data	X_2	X_1	X_1	X_1				X_1	
		flexible scheduling			X_2	X_2					
location requirements		easy access to storage facilities			X_3	X_2				X_2	
		transport links / infrastructure			X_2	X_2				X_2	
		acceptance of place of delivery		X_2	X_2	X_2				X_2	
Delivery requirements		supplier reliability			X_1	X_2	X_1	X_1	X_1	X_1	
		packaging and transport protection	X_2				X_2	X_2	X_2		
		deliver materials ready for production		X_1	X_1	X_2				X_1	
		top priority of orders					X_2	X_2	X_1		
		exclusive rights					X_2	X_2	X_1		
		supplier security	X_1			X_1	X_1	X_1	X_1	X_1	
Price requirements		willingness to analyse costs	X_1			X_1	X_2	X_2		X_1	
		price security	X_2			X_2				X_2	
		longer payment periods	X_2						X_3		
		leasing option	X_2								
		performance-related discount				X_2				X_2	
		no charges for small orders			X_2	X_2					
Service requirements		after-sales-service	X_1				X_1	X_1	X_1		
		recycling option	X_2	X_1	X_2	X_2	X_2	X_2	X_2	X_1	
		extended object guarantee	X_1			X_2					
		guaranteed follow-up orders				X_1					
		service capacity	X_3				X_3	X_3	X_3		
information requirements		information competence	X_2				X_1	X_1	X_1		
		willingness to provide information	X_2				X_1	X_1	X_1		
		willingness to solve problems	X_1				X_1	X_1	X_1		
		confidentiality					X_2	X_2	X_1		
		market information					X_2	X_2	X_2		
		application consulting	X_2				X_2	X_2	X_2		
		marketing cooperation					X_2	X_2			

Illustration 49: Supplier selection based on object characteristics (1)

The supplier is part of a market which he can influence only marginally. Although a supplier might look efficient and interesting, you might have to look for another, second-best supplier if his efficiency starts to decrease due to his environment. It is therefore necessary to examine your supplier´s environment thoroughly. Illustration 50 shows which factors of a supplier´s environment are important for which procurement objects.

Supplier selection criteria			singular product	cheap product	standard product	established product	top product	innovative product	purchaser-specific product	significance of quantity	etc.
Supplier criteria	Performance	work performance	X_1			X_2	X_1	X_1	X_1	X_2	
		management performance	X_1				X_1	X_1	X_1	X_2	
		technology	X_1				X_1	X_1	X_1		
		logistics performance		X_1	X_1					X_1	
		communication performance	X_1				X_1	X_1	X_1		
		capital performance			X_2	X_2				X_2	
		State's performance			X_2	X_2		X_3	X_3		
	Cost	labour costs	X_2	X_1	X_1	X_1	X_2	X_2	X_2	X_1	
		material costs		X_1	X_1	X_1	X_2	X_2	X_2	X_1	
		logistics costs		X_1	X_1	X_1				X_1	
		cost of capital		X_2	X_2	X_2				X_2	
		environmental charges		X_2	X_2	X_2	X_3	X_2	X_2	X_2	
		taxes and duties	X_2	X_2	X_2	X_2	X_3	X_2	X_2	X_2	
	Risk	dependance on imports		X_2		X_2				X_2	
		dependance on climate		X_1	X_1	X_1				X_1	
		political instability		X_2			X_1	X_2	X_2	X_1	
		strikes	X_1	X_2		X_1	X_1	X_1	X_1	X_1	
		economic instability	X_1	X_2		X_1	X_1	X_1	X_1	X_1	
		no possibility to use subsitute material					X_2	X_2	X_2		
		raw material speculations			X_2	X_2				X_2	

Conditions (object characteristics)

Illustration 50: Supplier selection based on object characteristics (2)

The assessment techniques which have been applied by purchasers so far tended to focus on the present, i.e. on the past. But it is essential to see potentials for tomorrow. Instead of taking a retrospective approach you should be dynamic and try to find innovative suppliers who are capable of and prepared to develop and improve performance levels (see Illustration 51).

88

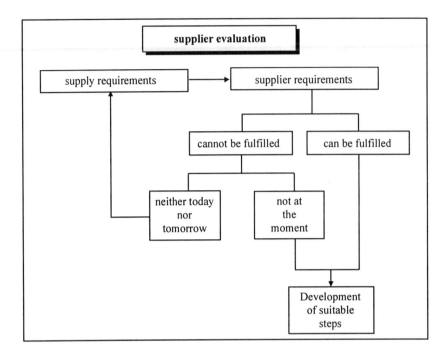

Illustration 51: Dynamic supplier evaluation and selection

When choosing such an approach you have to check what the input/output relation will be. Developing a supplier might be both risky and costly but it can be well worth the investment when handled properly.

The essential conclusion is that it is not only important to look after your *established* suppliers but to develop *new* suppliers as well.

4.5 Supplier Negotiations

The purchasing function has the target to fulfil corporate requirements economically by negotiating best possible prices with suppliers. In accordance with the coalition and contribution/incentive theories, however, both parties to a supply contract have to benefit from the results of their negotiations in the long-run. Otherwise win-win situations are hard to achieve. This means that the purchaser has the task to clarify

- which requirements have absolute priority;
- which requirements could be modified;

- which requirements could probably be neglected;
- which incentives are available to secure the cooperation of the supplier;
- which cost frame must be observed when giving suppliers incentives;
- which combination of incentives can be given at minimum costs without risking the required scope of supplies and services.

The process structure we have chosen provides a number of suitable answers in negotiating situations. In the negotiating stage the purchaser has to be able to act swiftly in order to secure corporate success.

4.51 Procurement Tools for Supplier Negotiations

Special marketing tools are widely used in sales marketing. Procurement, however, has not developed such a variety of tools and instruments yet. There is still a distinct lack of structure and alternative tools. This is particularly a problem when important pioneering work has to be done in procurement with regard to the identification and development of possible rooms for manoeuvre and areas of influence.

Let us look at a number of important prerequisites for developing a comprehensive set of procurement tools:

- Instrumental tools for the partners in the market are to be developed in accordance with one of the main marketing rules which says that marketing should always seek to solve problems of other parties in order to achieve its own goals.
- A transparent and comprehensive set of instrumental tools is to be designed. The structure which has to be developed therefore has to allow the integration of established tools as much as innovative new tools. If we could succeed in creating a structure of procurement tools which is similar to the tools used in marketing and sales, it would facilitate the use of such tools.
- Tools are to be developed on similar levels of abstraction. In sales we have defined tools, tool variables (i.e. policies) and tool variable effects (i.e. instruments) on three different levels of abstraction (see Koppelmann 1996, p. 475). This could be achieved in procurement too.

– A comprehensive set of tools has to be designed which provides as much room for manoeuvre in procurement as possible. Experience tells us that most purchasers tend to use a limited set of tools only. If you use a certain tool over and over again, however, you are more than likely to use it in situations in which other tools are much more appropriate. This is where alternative tools are called for.

– When developing procurement tools the principles of the incentive-contribution theory have to be observed. This is only possible if we develop both request tools and incentive tools. In most negotiating situations purchasers have to use both types of tools to achieve their targets.

When looking for suitable tools in procurement it is useful to look at the tools used in sales marketing. These tools, after all, are used by sales people to influence purchasers. It therefore seems possible to develop a corresponding set of procurement tools (see Illustration 52).

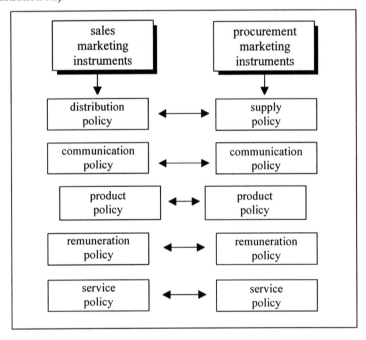

Illustration 52: Corresponding tools in sales and procurement

We can talk about supply policies here, with product policy being the key procurement tool variable.

When looking at individual tools we have to refer to the incentive-contribution principle again (see chapter 2.12). Based on the economic principle we must try to use tools in a way which does not only satisfy specific supply requirements at the lowest possible cost and price but gives the supplier crucial incentives as well. Consequently, it might seem appropriate to simply separate procurement tools in the two categories "request" and "incentive". We have decided against this option, however, as many procurement tools are ambiguos and can, under certain circumstances, have both qualities.

4.511 Product Policy

Illustration 53 shows a selection of tool variables and tool variable effects for product policies.

(1) The tool variable *product development policy* focuses on the novelty factor of a product as well as the decision who should develop new products. Tool variable effects are as follows:

– *in-house development*: the procurement object is developed by the purchaser himself;

– *supplier development*: the procurement object is developed by the supplier;

– *outsourced development*: the procurement object is developed by a specialized third party (i.e. neither the purchaser nor the supplier is involved);

– *partner development*: the procurement object is developed by purchaser and supplier and/or together with a third party;

– *new development*: the procurement object is a completely new development;

– *ongoing development*: the procurement object is continuously improved during production.

In-house development tends to be a request; this can be used as an incentive for the supplier if he does not have a R+D department or when he has no free research capacities and can rely on the buying company to observe his production standards. The same applies to supplier development: This tends to be an incentive as the supplier's capacities are used and he can adjust the development to his own production standards and methods. When the buying company does not have any R+D capacities, however, supplier development can be a request. If neither of the two parties have R+D functions at their disposal they can ask for development by a third party. From the supplier's point of view this request can actually be an incentive. Partner developments have both a request and an incentive quality. New developments certainly have a request character, no matter which party has to realize them. If the supplier has to realize the new development, it is a major incentive, especially if you consider how the supplier will gain from the new development. Ongoing development, i.e. improving products continuously, is certainly a request on part of the purchaser. It can be disruptive as far as the supplier's production processes are concerned, however, the supplier can benefit from a closer business relationship and a certain dependence of his customer.

	Product policy	

tool variable	tool variable effect	
	requests	incentives
product development policies	in-house development	
	very likely — in-house development — less probable	
	probable — supplier development — very likely	
	very likely — partner development — very likely	
	very likely — outsourced development — less probable	
	very likely — new development — very likely	
	very likely — ongoing development — less probable	
product design policies	very likely — design instructions — less probable	
	very likely — performance instructions — less probable	
	very likely — low design tolerances — less probable	
	very likely — buyer's brandname — less probable	
	less probable — supplier's brandname — very likely	
	very likely — product integration — less probable	
	less probable — product flexibility — very likely	
product manufacturing policies	very likely — low manufacturing tolerances — less probable	
	very likely — provisioning of materials — less probable	
	very likely — provisioning of tools — less probable	
product modification policies	very likely — product standardization — probable	
	probable — product differenciation — very likely	
	very likely — product updates — less probable	
	very likely — performance consistency — less probable	
	very likely — performance flexibility — very likely	
range of product policies	very likely — product selection — less probable	
	less probable — product mix — very likely	
product application policies	less probable — product design concessions — very likely	
	less probable — exclusive usage of products — very likely	

—— less probable   ——— probable   ———— very likely

Illustration 53: Product policies - tool variables and tool variable effects

(2) The tool variable *product design policy* provides the supplier with instructions and defines possible rooms for manoeuvre. Tool variable effects are as follows:

94

- *design instructions*: the product design is provided by the buying company in the form of drawings and technical specifications;

- *performance instructions*: a special paper defines the scope of supplies and performances to be fulfilled by the supplier; the supplier has considerable room for manoeuvre;

- *low design tolerances*: the designer has only limited room for manoeuvre when designing a product; suppliers are not normally given major room for manoeuvre here;

- *buyer's brandname*: the supplier is obliged to put the brandname/trademark of the customer on the procurement object;

- *supplier randname*: the supplier is entitled to put his own brandname/trademark on the procurement object;

- *product integration*: the supplier has to make sure that the design of the new procurement object matches the design of the buying company's other components and parts;

- *product flexibility*: the purchaser is prepared to accept the supplier's standard catalogue parts if the supplier cannot deliver the desired procurement object.

Design instructions as well as performance instructions certainly have a request quality. There is some leeway, however, as far as the strictness of the instructions is concerned. If you limit tolerances in design, you restrict your supplier significantly. When asking a supplier to put your brandname or trademark on a procurement object, you imply a depth of production you might not have. And you will most probably want the spare parts business to be handled by your own company. This has a strong request quality. On the other hand, it is a strong incentive to allow a supplier to put his own brandname or trademark on a product. When requiring that new procurement objects match existing products and components, you clearly demand more from a supplier than a one-off solution. Product flexibility means that the purchaser is prepared to try and meet his supply requirements by chosing from the supplier's established range of products.

(3) *Product manufacturing policies.* Manufacturing processes too require a set of request and incentive tools. Tool variable effects are as follows:

- *low manufacturing tolerance*: the production process has to guarantee that quality standards are maintained at all times;
- *provisioning of materials*: the supplier uses materials provided by the buying company;
- *provisioning of tools:* the supplier uses tools provided by the buying company

All tool variable effects mentioned above have a strong request quality.

(4) *Product modification policies* aim at altering and changing existing products:
- *product standardization*: instead of using a variety of special products a standardized procurement object is used;
- *product differenciation*: instead of using only one product, several products which fit the required function can be used. The supplier has to be able to provide several versions of such a product;
- *product updates*: the existing product is to be replaced regularly by up-dated versions;
- *product performance consistency*: consistent product performance is required at all times;
- *product performance flexibility*: the procurement object has to allow both higher and lower performance levels.

Product standardization has both an incentive and a request quality. When looking for possibilities to reduce costs for the customer, the supplier can benefit from cost degression effects. This, however, is only attractive for the supplier if he can increase orders booked considerably, for example by becoming a preferred supplier. When seeking to differenciate existing products, you give your suppliers a strong incentive as this usually leads to increased profits. The buying company, however, may become more dependent on the supplier. Product updates can be necessary, e.g., when you want to re-launch a product with a slightly changed design. This tends to be a request. The supplier might require new equipment, tools and procedures. Product performance consistency too is a request on part of the buying company. Product performance flexibility, on the other hand, offers the possibility to increase or decrease performance levels of a product. This can be both a request and an incentive.

(5) *Product range policies* include the following tool variable effects:
- *product selection*: only a number of interesting products is selected from the existing range of products;
- *product mix*: the purchaser buys a major part of the supplier's existing range of products.

Product selection clearly has a request quality while product mix provides a major incentive for the supplier.

(6) *Product application policies* encompass the following tool variable effects:
- *product design concessions*: the supplier is granted certain concessions concerning the further processing of a product;
- *exclusive usage of products*: the supplier is granted certain concessions concering the exclusive usage of the procurement object in special end products.

Both tool variable effects are very attractive incentives when the supplier is not really interested in a deal or if he is interested in vertical quality managment or wants to get into the buying company's market.

All procurement tools described above need to be checked and updated permanently.

4.512 Service Policy

Illustration 54 indicates possible tool variables and tool variable effects for service policies.

tool variable	tool variable effects		
	requests		**incentives**
supplier support policies		research and development support	▬
		design support	▬
		production support	▬
		procurement support	▬
		sales support	▬
		finance support	▬
delivery service policies	▬	delivery	
		collection	▬
	▬	ability to deliver	
	▬	supply reliability	
		acceptance of delivery	▬
		order volume reliability	▬
	▬	supply quality guarantee	
		acceptance tolerance	▬
customer-service policies	▬	production-specific adjustments	▬
	▬	sales-specific adjustments	▬
	▬	assembly / development / testing	
	▬	maintenance / repairs / servicing	▬
	▬	provisioning of spare parts	▬
	▬	staff support	
	▬	provisioning of materials	
	▬	after-sales service support	▬
	▬	recycling support	▬
guarantee policies	▬	scope of guarantee	
	▬	warrenty and guarantee period	
	▬	warrenty and guarantee performances	
	▬	goodwill	
performance assurance policies	▬	quality audits	▬
	▬	quality documentation	▬
	▬	progress reports	▬
	▬	Total-Quality-Management	▬

▬ less probable   ▬ probable   ▬ very likely

Illustration 54: Service policies - tool variables and tool variable effects

(1) By pursuing a *supplier support policy* the purchaser supports the supplier in

- *research and development*
- *construction and design*
- *production*
- *procurement*
- *sales*
- *finance*
- *etc*

This kind of function-related support can be given both through planning and tools, including materials, services and staff capacities. Planning support is of particular importance where system sourcing strategies are pursued. In price negotiations, e.g., a lot of purchasers simply request price reductions of up to 30 per cent instead of considering mutual ways of achieving such reductions together. In the automotive industry a new approach has lead to completely new forms of cooperation between customers and suppliers. Supplier support is an enormous incentive.

Services tools can focus on the flow of information and have a strong advisory aspect (know-how transfer are part of communication policies). Services can include much more, however, if you assess service tools according to their request and incentive quality.

(2) *Delivery service policies* focus on how a procurement objects reaches the buying company:

- *delivery*: the procurement object is delivered to a place (warehouse, production site) named by the purchaser;
- *collection*: the purchaser or a third party commissioned by the purchaser collects the procurement object at the supplier's site;
- *ability to deliver*: the supplier is able to deliver the requested procurement object at the stipulated time;
- *supply reliability*: the supplier has to observe stipulated delivery dates, quantities,

qualities and places;

- *acceptance of delivery*: the purchaser has to accept procurement objects upon delivery;
- *order volume reliability*: the purchaser actually places orders in the promised quantities and qualities;
- *supply quality guarantee*: the supplier guarantees the continuous quality of the ordered goods;
- *acceptance tolerance*: the purchaser tolerates minor faults of the delivered goods.

All the tool variable effects mentioned above reflect mutual efforts to reduce costs, with the incentive and request qualities being more differenciated. Stipulating places and terms of delivery is normally a request, offering to collect goods an incentive. The ability to deliver, supply reliability and supply quality guarantee are requests on part of the purchaser while acceptance of delivery, order volume reliability and acceptance tolerance are incentives he can give his supplier.

(3) The tool variable effects of *customer service policies* are well known:
- *production-specific adjustments*: the procurement object is supplied in such a form and way that it can enter the production process directly;
- *sales-specific adjustments*: the procurement project is supplied in such a way that it can be resold without any modifications;
- *assembly / development / testing*: assembly, development and testing are the responsibility of the supplier;
- *maintenance/ repairs / servicing*: the supplier is obliged to perform maintenance, repairs and services at set intervalls;
- *provisioning of spare parts*: the supplier must guarantee that spare parts are supplied adequately and without delay for a stipulated period of time;
- *staff support*: the supplier supports the purchaser by providing experienced staff when bottlenecks and problems arise;
- *materials provisioning*: the supplier supports the purchaser by providing materials

when bottlenecks and problems arise;

– *after sales service support*: the purchaser provides the after-sales services for the supplier;

– *recycling support*: the supplier is responsible for adequate recycling and waste disposal.

Some of the above mentioned tool variable effects correspond with supplier support policies. They tend to have both a request and an incentive quality. Production-specific adjustments are a request. But if a supplier has the appropriate equipment for realizing such adjustments, it can be an incentive for him to be given the chance to use it. The same applies to sales-related adjustments (e.g. flexible packaging lines). While assembly, developments and testing are certainly demands on part of the purchaser, maintenance, repairs and after-sales services are usually very profitable incentives for the supplier. The provisioning of spare parts is often a request on part of the purchaser and can be a burden for the supplier unless he can negotiate acceptable prices. Staff support and the provisioning of materials are clearly requests on part of the purchaser. If the buying company provides after-sales services itself, however, it might actually take a burden off the supplier's shoulders, especially as far as special components and high-tech parts are concerned. After-sales services can prove to be highly profitable for the buying company. As long as recycling requires a lot of research and administration, the purchaser will request the support of his supplier, especially if the supplier is experienced in this field.

(4) *Guarantee and warranty policies* are well known in the sales function:

– *scope of guarantee*: the supplier guarantees a certain scope of supplies and services;

– *warranty and guarantee period*: the supplier agrees to stipulated warrantee and guarantee periods;

– *warranty and guarantee performances*: the supplier agrees to fulfil the required warranty and guarantee performances;

– *goodwill*: when disputes arise the supplier is requested to show goodwill.

Goodwill is certainly difficult to request or enforce, however, most purchasers regard it as an important issue. All the above mentioned points have a strong request quality.

(5) *Performance assurance policies* are gaining in importance in view of Total Quality Management and Just-in-Time production:

- *quality audits*: the supplier is obliged to take appropriate steps to secure quality standards;
- *quality documentation*: the supplier is obliged to provide a full documentation of the steps taken to secure quality standards;
- *Total Quality Management*: the supplier is obliged to realize a comprehensive total quality concept;
- *schedule control*: the supplier is obliged to provide progress reports regularly and to make sure that no problems arise in production schedules.

Most of the points mentioned above are requests. Suppliers which can provide all these tool variable effects have a considerable advantage over their competitors.

4.513 Supply Policy

Illustration 55 illustrates tool variables and tool variable effects for suppy policies

tool variable	tool variable effect		
	requests		**incentives**
supply quantity policies	▬▬ / ▬ / ▬▬ / ▬▬	small order quantity / large order quantity / variable order quantity / exact order quantity	▬ / ▬▬▬ / ▬ / ▬
procurement organization policies	▬ / ▬ / ▬ / ▬ / ▬ / ▬▬ / ▬	centralized purchasing / decentralized purchasing / purchasing offices / local puchasers / purchasing agents / purchasing cooperation / cooperation in waste management	▬ / ▬ / ▬▬ / ▬▬ / ▬▬ / ▬ / ▬
supply-contract policies	▬ / ▬▬ / ▬▬ / ▬▬ / ▬▬ / ▬▬ / ▬ / ▬ / ▬▬ / ▬▬ / ▬	framework agreement / subcontracting / consignment stock / exclusive rights / capacity booking / fixed deals / delivery ex works / carrier acceptance terms / cost acceptance terms / destination acceptance terms / recycling of materials	▬▬▬ / ▬▬ / ▬▬ / ▬▬ / ▬ / / ▬▬▬ / ▬▬▬ / ▬ / ▬ / ▬▬
logistical policies	▬▬ / ▬▬ / ▬▬ / ▬▬▬ / ▬▬ / ▬▬ / ▬▬	central storage facilities / decentralized storage facilities / external storage facilities / stipulated means of transport / stipulated carrier / stipulated routes of transport / stipulated means of communication	▬▬ / ▬▬ / ▬▬ / ▬▬ / ▬▬▬ / ▬▬ / ▬▬

▬ less probable ▬▬ probable ▬▬▬ very likely

Illustration 55: Supply policies - tool variables and tool variable effects

(1) *Supply quantity policy* is the quantity-related part of product policies, however, we want to focus on the supply aspect here. While the supply quantity defines the total volume of a procurement object per planning period, the order quantity is merely the part of the total volume which the supplier has to deliver at a certain time. In case of deliveries on call the order quantity is split in several part shipments to be sent to the purchaser at a time.

Tool variable effects of supply quantity policies are as follows:

— *small order quantities*: the supplier has to be able to supply small quantities;

— *large order quantities*: the supplier has to able to supply large quantities;

— *variable order quantities*: the supplier has to be able to deliver both small and large quantities;

— *exact order quantities*: the supplier has to deliver exactly the quantity ordered.

Placing small orders with a supplier has a request character, especially if the supplier is in a position to deliver bigger quantities. Ordering large quantities requires that the supplier has corresponding capacities and is therefore a request on part of the purchaser. When large orders result in a better usage of existing capacities of the supplier, they can be a major incentive. Variable order quantities tend to be a request for higher flexibility on part of the supplier. They can be an incentive as well when you give your supplier preference over other sources and offer him interesting order volumes. Asking a supplier to deliver exact quantities only is a request. Effective and continuos quantity planning can result in a considerable reduction of inventory levels and lower the risk of disruptions in production.

(2) *Procurement organization policies* address the question which departments, functions or individuals are best suited for establishing cooperation with suppliers.

— *centralized purchasing departments*: all procurement activities and operations are handled in-house by a centralized purchasing department. In large groups of companies such centralized purchasing departments are usually responsible for concluding and managing framework agreements with suppliers;

— *decentralized purchasing departments*: all procurement activities and operations are handled directly at the sites (workshops, plants, etc) where demands arise;

- *purchasing offices*: procurement activities and operations are initiated and managed directly by purchasing offices the company has established in the respective supply markets;
- *local purchasers*: the company employs individual purchasers who cultivate the contacts with suppliers in their own countries;
- *purchasing agents*: when there is a special demand situation the company hires independent purchasing agents who have a thorough knowledge of a country, region or line of business;
- *purchasing cooperation/consortiums*: several buying companies join forces and co-ordinate their procurement activities and operations;
- *cooperation in waste disposal and recycling*: the buying and the selling company work together on suitable ways for the recycling and disposal of waste.

A centralized purchasing department can be both a request and an incentive. Such a department can coordinate material demands, define strategies, negotiate framework agreements and design a suitable set of procurement tools. Staff in centralized purchasing departments have to have a high level of competence and authority. Depending on its internal organisation such a department can be either flexible and swift or inefficient and bureaucratical in its reactions and operations. Staff in decentralized purchasing departments require more specialized know-how, have a thorough knowledge of concrete situations and demands, and are often responsible for materials planning and scheduling too. Special purchasing offices which are located near the suppliers' sites can provide a special incentive as they can help to overcome cultural and communication barriers. The purchaser in the market could actually initiate some sales activities for his supplier and secure orders for him. Employing individual purchasers for operating in a market can be the first step towards establishing entire purchasing offices in that market. Local purchasers can either come from the country in question or be sent by headquarters. One of their essential tasks is to assist the company's other purchasers in sourcing activities. Purchasing agents are often self-employed and do not cause any or only minor fixed costs. They have the necessary contacts in different markets and know potential suppliers. Although they might be difficult to control and manage, they can be of great assistance to the purchaser. Purchasing consortiums are mainly established in the trade sector to use synergies and increase purchasing power. This has a request quality. The supplier has to be prepared to cooperate with the consortium, the individual members of which want to become more attractive for their mutual suppliers. It can be a major incentive for the supplier to work for such a consortium if he is interested in bigger order volumes. Cooperation in the field of waste disposal and recycling can be both a request and an incentive, depending on the quantity of waste and recycling material and the relevant regulations concerning the handling of such materials.

(3) Supply contract policies deal with different types of supply contracts:

- *framework agreement*: procurement objects as well as terms and conditions are fixed in an agreement. Quantities and schedules are specified in accordance with corporate demands; order rhythm mechanisms can be used;

- *subcontracting*: the buying company stipulates from which subsuppliers goods and materials have to be obtained;

- *consignment stock*: the supplier is obliged to keep the procurement object in question on stock in a warehouse nearby the buying company. The buying company is entitled to satisfy corporate demands by taking materials from this stock;

- *exclusive contract*: the supplier is not entitled to deliver goods or services to any other company;

- *capacity booking*: the supplier reserves certain production capacities for the buying company so as to be in a position to meet urgent and unexpected demands without delay;

- *fixed deals*: the supplier agrees to deliver the goods at a fixed date. In case of a delay the buying company reserves the right to cancel the order and/or make the supplier responsible for any losses incurred;

- *delivery ex works* (INCOTERMS 1990): the buying company collects the goods at the supplier's site and bears the cost and risk of transport;

- *carrier acceptance terms* (INCOTERMS, F-group): the supplier delivers the pro
curement objects to the carrier (free carrier, free alongside ship, free on board) and
the buying company pays for the major part of transport;
- *cost acceptance terms* (INCOTERMS, C-group): the supplier hires the forwarding
agent, pays all costs from his site to, e.g., the port of destination and bears all risks
till the moment the consignment passes the ship's rail when being loaded on board;
- *destination acceptance terms* (INCOTERMS, D-group): the procurement object can
be delivered to the border, on board ship or on quay in the port of destination, or to
the customer's site in the country of destination;
- *recycling of materials*: the buying company is entitled to return any waste or recycling material to the supplier.

Framework agreements are certainly an incentive for a supplier as they give him the
chance to plan his production and capacities over a longer period of time. Subcontracting is a request as the supplier's room for manoeuvre is fairly limited. If a supplier
is not very experienced in procurement, this can be considered an incentive as well,
however. Asking a supplier to carry consignment stock for his customer is certainly a
strong request. The incentive for the supplier is that higher inventory levels may lead
to higher usage of the stored parts. The conclusion of exclusive contracts is a strong
request. The supplier benefits from increased order quantities and the fact that the
customer is not likely to change to another supplier. Reserving production capacities
for a customer is a similar request. The purchaser books production capacities without
being absolutely certain that he will actually use these capacities. The incentive for the
supplier is the fee to be paid by the buying company when the reserved capacities are
not used as well as a strong link to the customer. Fixed deals are clearly requests on
part of the customer. Deliveries ex-works as well as the F-terms of the INCOTERMS
are strong incentives for the supplier as the purchaser bears all cost and risks of transport. The C and D terms of the INCOTERMS, however, are strong requests on part of
the customer. The handling of recycling and waste disposal can be a strong request

and, if the supplier has the right facilities, an incentive as well.

(4) Logistical policies: Whether logistics is actually a responsibility of the procurement department or not, it is an issue that needs to be addressed here. Possible tool variable effects are:

– *central storage facilities*: the supplier delivers to a central storage facility of the buying company;

– *decentralized storage facilities*: the supplier delivers to the individual production sites of the buying company;

– *external storage facilities*: the supplier delivers to the storage facilities of a third party;

– *stipulated means of transport*: the purchaser stipulates the means of transport to be used;

– *stipulated carrier*: the purchaser stipulates which carrier or forwarder has to handle transport;

– *stipulated route of transport*: the purchaser stipulates which transport route the carrier has to take;

– *stipulated means of communication*: the purchaser stipulates which hardware and software are to be used for all relevant communication concerning transport and logistics.

For the supplier it is normally less expensive to deliver goods to a central storage facility than to a lot of decentralized warehouses. If a company has an efficient distribution system (like most trading companies), this can be of considerable importance. Asking your supplier to deliver goods to the storage facilities of a third party is not a critical request as it normally does not cause major additional costs, the only possible difference being distance and technical means. It is a request, however, when purchasers ask to use such storage facilities in outsourcing projects. Stipulated means of transport, carriers, forwarders and transport routes are requests on part of the buyer which can be incentives for the supplier if based on mutual agreement. The same applies to stipulating special means of communication. The supplier might have to adjust to the purchaser's requests at first, but once the new means of communication have been implemented, he will clearly benefit from the changes.

4.514 Remuneration Policy

One of the most important procurement tools in every-day business is the remuneration policy. How can I get my supplier to reduce his "best" prices? Often buyers presume - more or less openly - that the supplier will somehow manage to make up for his loss by increasing prices for other customers, and preferably for the buying company's competitors. Win-win situations are nowhere in sight here. Illustration 56 shows the choice of possibilities you have for remuneration policies.

(1) *Price policy*: The purchaser can choose from a wide range of tool variable effects in daily business.

- *price pressure*: the purchaser seeks to cut prices to the bone;
- *attractive prices*: the purchaser seeks to get the supplier to deliver goods or service by paying him attractive prices;
- *target prices*: the purchaser sets a target price based on his own calculations;
- *price acceptance*: the purchaser is willing to make certain concessions and accept the prices requested by the supplier;
- *performance-related prices*: when contractual supply requirements are changed, supplier and purchaser are both entitled to adjust prices accordingly;
- *competition-related prices*: the purchaser asks the supplier to adjust his prices to the price level of his competitors;
- *fixed prices*: for a set period of time a price is fixed which is not affected by any market developments;
- *price adjustments*: purchaser and supplier agree how to adjust prices to changed market conditions.

tool variable	tool variable effect		
	requests		incentives
price policies	very likely	price pressure	
		attractive prices	very likely
	probable	target prices	less probable
		price acceptance	probable
	less probable	performance-related prices	probable
	very likely	competition-related prices	less probable
	probable	fixed prices	probable
	less probable	price adjustments	very likely
discount policies	probable	quantity discount	
	very likely	first order / regular order discount	
	probable	special discount	
	probable	cash discount	
	very likely	no additional charges for small order volumens	
bonus policies		priority bonus	very likely
		quantity bonus	very likely
		time bonus	very likely
		special service bonus	very likely
penalty policies	probable		
payment term policies	probable	payment institutions	less probable
	probable	payment modus	less probable
	probable	payment schedule	less probable
	probable	payment currency	less probable
	less probable	payment guarantee	very likely
credit policies		supplier credit allowance	very likely
	probable	supplier credit request	
	probable	acquisition of company shares	very likely

— less probable　　━━━ probable　　━━━━ very likely

Illustration 56: Remuneration policies - tool variables and tool variable effects

Price pressure is clearly a request on part of the purchaser while attractive prices are a major incentive for the supplier. One possible scenario when starting a business relationship is to pursue an attractive price policy first and then to gradually exert pressure on prices with a view to market developments. Target prices are usually requests. The purchaser can, for example, conduct a purchase cost analysis and calculate an opti-

110

mum price for the procurement object in question. This price is then presented to the supplier as the target price. Or the purchaser can apply target costing methods (see Seidenschwarz, 1993, and references indicated therein) and break down the costs of every single procurement object, thus calculating cost ceilings: as the procurement object in question is not allowed to be more expensive, design and production have to be adjusted accordingly. Price acceptance, on the other hand, is an incentive for the supplier as the purchaser is willing to make compromises and meet the supplier half-way when talking about prices. Performance-related prices are incentives too as any alterations in the scope of supplies and services influence the prices directly. Asking your supplier to adjust his prices to the prices of his competitors is a strong request. If your suppplier already offers the lowest prices in the market, however, this request can be used as an incentive. Fixed prices help both the purchaser and the supplier to plan their prices ahead. Price adjustments are both an incentive and a request as long as suitable adjustment mechanisms have been mutually agreed upon.

(2) *Price discount policies* are especially important in the trading sector. In the industrial sector quantity discounts are the most common discounts.
– *quantity discount*: the purchaser ask for discounts for the order volumes placed;
– *first order/ regular ordering discount*: the purchaser asks for a discount off the list prices for placing orders for the first respectively the umpteenth time;
– *special service discount*: the purchaser requests a discount for any special services performed by him;
– *cash discount*: the purchaser asks for a price discount for paying his bills within a short time;
– *no additional charges for small order volumes*: the supplier is not entitled to claim any additional charges if the purchaser places small order volumes.

Price discounts are always requests on part of the purchaser.

(3)   *Bonus policies* are pursued by the purchaser in order to give the supplier special incentives. The idea is to pay the supplier a special sum in addition to the sales price.

- *priority bonus*: the supplier gets a special bonus for giving top priority to the orders of the buying company;
- *quantity bonus*: the supplier gets a special bonus for supplying unexpected or adjusted order quantities;
- *time bonus*: the supplier gets a bonus for accepting unexpected or adjusted delivery schedules;
- *special service bonus*: the supplier gets a bonus for rendering additional services for the purchaser which were not part of the initial agreement.

(4) *Penalty policies* are pursued to deal with the supplier's failure to fulfil his contractual obligations. In most fixed orders penalties are agreed for cases of delays in delivery. Penalty agreements, however, can be fixed for other contractual stipulations as well. Penalties are a strong request on part of the purchaser.

(5) *Terms of payment policies* are especially important for international purchasing operations:

- *payment institution*: the purchaser stipulates that all financial transactions are to be realized through a certain financial institution / bank;
- *payment modus*: the purchaser decides which way the supplier will get his money;
- *payment schedule*: the purchaser decides when he will pay his supplier's bills;
- *payment currency*: the purchaser decides in which currency he will settle his bills;
- *payment guarantee*: the purchaser gives the supplier certain guarantees that he can settle his bills when due.

Apart from the payment guarantee, which is a clear incentive for the supplier, all other tool variable effects mentioned above are requests on part of the purchaser. When trying to reach a compromise with his supplier, the purchaser can decide how and whether to use these requests.

(6) *Credit policies* have to be pursued when the financial situation of your supplier or of your own company is not sufficiently secure for concluding a business deal:

- *supplier credit allowance*: the purchaser grants his supplier a credit;
- *supplier credit request*: the purchaser asks his supplier for a "credit" by requesting longer periods for the settlement of outstanding bills.
- *acquisition of company shares / investments*: both buying and supplying company have the possibility to invest directly in the other company, for example by ac-quiring shares of each other.

The incentive and request qualities of the tool effect variables mentioned above do not need to be explained in detail.

4.515 Communication Policy

In future, communications policies will be growing more in importance than other ar-eas. The complexity of corporate activities as well as the scope of communication in-crease considerably when you start looking into optimizing the process chain within your company and towards your supplier, when you outsource more and more corpo-rate activities, when you pursue simultaneous engineering strategies or decide to im-plement modular and system sourcing strategies. New communication technology is available which can be used effectively in procurement.

Illustration 57 shows tool variables and tool variable effects for communication poli-cies

tool variable	Communication policy		
	tool variable effects		
	requests		incentives
contact policies	▬▬▬▬ ▬▬▬▬ ▬▬▬▬ ▬ ▬▬▬▬	openess competence suitable media buyer's trade fairs supplier discussion days	▬▬▬▬ ▬▬▬▬ ▬▬▬▬ ▬▬▬▬ ▬▬▬▬
procurement process handling	▬▬▬▬ ▬▬▬▬ ▬▬▬▬ ▬▬▬▬	offer handling feedback to (rejected) offers orders and order cancellation invoicing complaints and disputes	▬▬▬▬ ▬▬▬▬ ▬▬▬▬ ▬▬▬▬
know-how transfer policies	▬▬▬▬ ▬▬▬▬ ▬▬▬▬ ▬▬▬▬ ▬▬▬	problem communication confidentiality market information product application advice consulting services	▬▬▬▬ ▬▬▬▬ ▬▬▬▬ ▬
reference policies	▬▬▬▬ ▬▬▬	supplier's references buyer's references third party references	▬▬▬ ▬▬▬▬ ▬▬▬
advertising policies	▬ ▬ ▬▬▬▬	supplier competitions advertising on demands direct advertising	▬▬▬▬ ▬▬▬▬ ▬▬▬▬

▬ less probable   ▬▬▬▬ probable   ▬▬▬▬▬ very likely

Illustration 57: Communication policies - tool variables and tool variable effects

(1) *Contact policies* address the question how to establish contacts with new suppliers and cultivate existing buyer-supplier relationships.

– *openess*: buyer and supplier are both open to the other party´s ideas and suggestions (concerning problems, schedules, etc);

– *competence*: buyer and supplier delegate competent people for mutual tasks;

– *suitable media*: buyer and supplier provide suitable media for communication;

– *buyer´s trade fairs and presentations*: the buyer presents the parts and components he would like to purchase;

– *supplier discussion days*: the buyer invites the supplier to discuss mutual problems.

Openess, competence and suitable media are both requests and incentives for buyer and supplier. Failures will upset the equilibrium considerably. Buyer's trade fairs are usually organized with other companies which operate in the same market or region. Company-specific presentations offer suppliers the opportunity to do some research in a market without major expenses on their part. After the initial contact has been established and information has been exchanged the purchaser will naturally expect the individual supplier to call on him personally. Supplier discussion days give suppliers the chance to understand procurement problems and develop suitable solutions together with the purchaser.

(2) *Procurement process handling:* There are many problems in the handling of procurement processes. Quite often sales contracts are concluded which are not actually legally binding. The results can be endless discussions and enquiries, complaints and adjustments which are both time and money consuming.

– *offer handling*: the purchaser gives precise instructions which have to be observed by the supplier when submitting an offer;

– *reaction to offers*: the purchaser is obliged to explain why an offer might not be acceptable or attractive for him, thus giving the supplier the chance to make the necessary adjustments and win future orders;

– *orders and cancellation of orders*: purchaser and supplier agree on mutually acceptable ways of ordering and cancelling orders;

– *invoicing*: purchaser and supplier agree on a transparent way of invoicing and charging taxes, duties, packaging costs, etc;

– *settlement of complaints / disputes*: purchaser and supplier agree on special procedures for settling complaints and legal disputes.

Instructing your supplier how to submit his offers is clearly a request while your feedback on his offers is an incentive for the supplier. All tool variable effects mentioned above can be used both as requests and incentives.

(3)   *Know-how transfer policies:* It is vital that companies give up their secrecy when dealing with other companies and establish relationships based on openess and trust. If you want to develop your suppliers against the background of product policies you will need open communication:

– *communication of problems*: purchaser and supplier exchange information about current problems;

– *secrecy agreements*: the business parners make special secrecy agreements about the flow of information and take appropriate steps to ensure that information is handled confidentially;

– *market information*: purchaser and supplier provide each other with any relevant market information they might have;

– *product application advice*: the purchaser expects from his supplier advice on the best use and application of his products;

– *consulting services*: the purchaser expects from the suppliers consulting services and advice for other corporate functions as well.

The communication of problems as well as secrecy agreements are both requests and incentives, depending on who provides what kind of information. The same applies to the communication of market information. The purchaser can save costs for sourcing activities while the supplier can save costs for market research. Asking for advice on the use and application of products, however, is more a request on part of the purchaser. This can be an incentive if the supplier has special personnel for that purpose and can get relevant information and contacts in return. In the present context we have defined consulting services as a request only in order to differenciate it from supplier support in service policies.

(4) *Reference policies:* When changing your established supplier or when selecting a new supplier for a new procurement object there is always a certain risk involved. This is the more critical when you are seeking to establish long-lasting business relationships with selected suppliers.

- *supplier's references*: the purchaser asks his supplier for trade references of other customers in comparable supply situations.
- *buyer's references*: the purchaser provides the supplier with references of other suppliers in comparable supply situations.
- *third party references*: a third, neutral party (e.g. a bank) provides references on both purchaser and supplier.

It is quite obvious that asking your supplier for references is a request, providing your supplier with references is an incentive and getting references from a third party is both a request and an incentive.

(5) *Advertising policies:* In the industrial sector advertising policies are not regarded as being as important as in the consumer goods market:

- *supplier competitions*: when seeking to ensure absolutely impeccable quality levels, purchasers can start special competitions for their suppliers and award the winners; the suppliers can use these awards for advertising purposes;
- *advertising of demands*: when launching into new markets purchasers can advertise their demand for specific procurement objects, for example, in newspapers and magazines, thus attracting potential suppliers; when drafting the advert, the purchaser has the option to include information on what he can offer the supplier in return for his services and supplies;
- *direct advertising*: the purchaser may ask the supplier to start a marketing and advertising campaign aimed directly at the purchaser's customers.

While supplier competitions and the advertising of demands are incentives for the supplier, direct advertising is a request. However, it can be an incentive as well if the end product has a very good reputation in the market.

4.52 Combination of Procurement Tools (Procurement Tool Mix)

Not all procurement tools can be used with the same efficiency at all times - they are to be regarded as alternatives which have to be applied in the right situation. You have to keep in mind that the effectiveness of individual tools might be reduced and that some tools might be completely ineffective when they are combined with other procurement tools. On the other hand, you have to look for possibilities to increase the effectiveness of the applied procurement tools and seek to achieve synergy effects. We want to focus on these potentials here.

After having defined a set of suitable procurement tools you have to look for a way to observe the economic principle, i.e. you have to make sure that the tools are combined in a way which allows the realization of your procurement targets at the lowest possible costs.

Illustration 58 gives a very simplified view of the structure of selecting procurement tools.

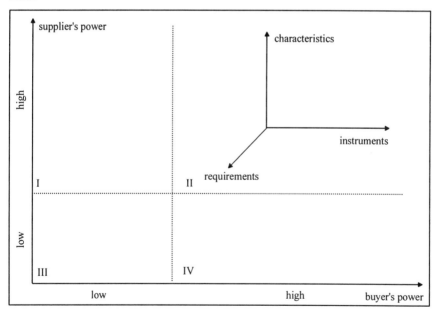

Illustration 58: Structured selecting of procurement tools

118

In a given situation it depends entirely on your intended targets what the best combination of request and incentive tool variables and tool variable effects might be. Although it might be possible to allocate some procurement targets and procurement tools directly, such an allocation would require considerable research and decision-making efforts and destroy the quality of the overall set of procurement tools. On a higher level of abstraction we would like to define synergical tool combinations and recommend them for specific procurement situations. To this end we can refer to procurement object characteristics again and focus on selecting corresponding tool variable effects. The correlation between supply requirements and object characteristics (see chapter 4.23) provides us with the information which procurement object characteristics call for which supply requirements.

The complexity of the issue has thus been reduced and influences the tool combination process. We need to be able to anticipate how difficult or easy it is going to be to satisfy corporate requirements by making requests and giving incentives to our suppliers.

Illustration 59 illustrates the decision-making process required for combining procurement tools effectively.

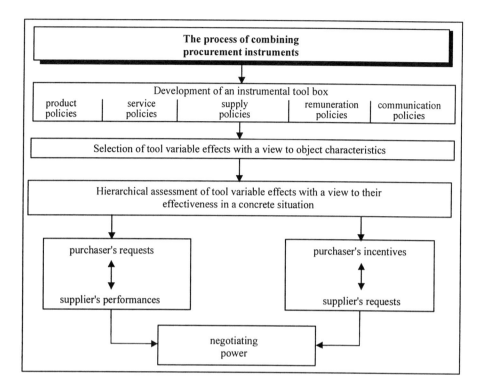

Illustration 59: Combination of procurement tools

In the following matrixes we will illustrate the suitability of individual procurement tools and test their effectiveness. These matrixes are not the result of empirical tests but of extensive discussions with procurement managers and purchasers. As the new approches are yet to be implemented it would have been premature to conduct surveys and a systematical analysis at this stage.

Through the discussions an empirically-tested level of plausibility has been established. In a given corporate demand situation it has to be decided whether the recommended combination of tools would be viable and effective or whether it needs to be adjusted.

A high suitability (x_1) of a procurement tool variable indicates that it is considered absolutely necessary, i.e. a *must* variable, while a low assessment (x_3) indicates that that tool variable could be abandoned. The assessment of a tool variable as *can* variable (x_2) indicates that it is an option which might be useful but not absolutely necessary. In order to simplify the terminology we will talk about *instruments* in the following instead of using the more exact term *variable tool effects*.

(1) Suitability of procurement instruments for product policies

Illustration 60 shows procurement instruments for product policies in an hierarchical order.

Product policies	tool variable and tool variable effects	singular product	cheap product	standard product	established product	top product	innovative product	purchaser-specific product	quantity significance	etc.
product development policies	in-house development					x_1	x_1	x_1	x_2	
	supplier development	x_1	x_1			x_1	x_1	x_1	x_2	
	partner development	x_2				x_1	x_1	x_1	x_2	
	outsourced development	x_2				x_2	x_2	x_2	x_3	
	new development	x_1	x_2			x_1	x_1	x_1	x_2	
	ongoing development		x_2		x_2	x_2	x_2	x_2	x_2	
product design policies	design instructions	x_2	x_2			x_1	x_2	x_2	x_2	x_1
	performance instructions	x_1	x_1			x_1	x_1	x_1	x_1	x_1
	low design tolerances	x_2	x_2			x_1	x_1	x_1	x_1	x_1
	buyer's brandname					x_2	x_2	x_2	x_2	
	supplier's brandname					x_2	x_2	x_2	x_2	
	product consistency		x_2			x_1	x_1	x_1	x_1	x_1
	product flexibility	x_2	x_2			x_1	x_1			x_2
product manufacturing policies	low manufacturing tolerance		x_2			x_1	x_1	x_1	x_1	x_1
	provisioning of materials	x_3				x_2				x_2
	provisioning of tools					x_2	x_2	x_2		
product modification policies	product standardization		x_1			x_2				x_1
	product differenciation					x_2	x_3	x_2		
	product updates					x_2	x_2	x_2	x_2	
	performance continuity	x_2	x_2	x_1	x_1	x_1	x_1	x_1	x_1	
	performance flexibility					x_2	x_2	x_2	x_1	
range of products policies	product selection					x_2	x_2			
	product mix					x_3	x_3	x_3	x_2	
product application policies	product design concession					x_1	x_2			
	product application concessions					x_2	x_2			

Illustration 60: Hierarchy of procurement instruments for product policies

When discussing the procurement object characteristics (if-conditions) of "singular products" purchasing experts agreed that the factors supplier development (in-house development did not seem a viable solution in most cases), new development (to secure state-of-the-art) and performance instructions (some said, e.g., that in a machine the output performance was more important than the way how this performance was achieved) were essential requirements, while other factors such as partner development or development through third parties, design instructions, low design tolerances, product integration and product adjustments as well as product performance consistency were not critical issues.

When examining other procurement object characteristics correspondingly, a few points are bound to attract your attention :

- There are some procurement instruments which are generally classified as being of relatively low importance (e.g. product selection and product mix policies).

- There are some procurement instruments which are generally regarded as very important (e.g. product performance consistency and performance instructions).

- With some procurement object characteristics (e.g. top product and innovative product) the available set of instruments and tools is used extensively, while others (e.g. singular product and standard product) do not seem to attract a comprehensive use of procurement tools.

(2) Suitability of procurement instruments for service policies

It seems that procurement instruments which can be used in supplier support policies are not given great importance in every-day business, the only exceptions being design support and R+D support for special products. As far as supply policies are concerned the general opinion seems to vary between "important" and "not so important". The same applies to performance assurance policies where opinions differ greatly. The only instruments which are commonly regarded as "suitable" are production-specific adjustments and recycling support. Most customer service policies as well as guarantee and warranty policies are considered important as far as performance-related characteristics and singular products are concerned (see Illustration 61).

122

tool variables and tool variable effects			singular product	cheap product	standard product	established product	top product	innovative product	purchaser-specific product	quantity significance	etc.
Service policy	supplier support policies	research and development support	X_3				X_2	X_2	X_1		
		design support					X_1	X_1	X_1	X_2	
		manufacturing support		X_2		X_2	X_2	X_2	X_2	X_2	
		procurement support		X_2		X_2	X_2	X_2	X_2	X_2	
		sales support	X_3	X_3		X_2	X_2	X_2	X_2	X_2	
		finance support	X_3				X_2	X_2	X_2	X_2	
	delivery service policies	delivery	X_1	X_2	X_2	X_1	X_2	X_2	X_2	X_1	
		collection					X_2	X_2	X_2	X_2	
		ability to deliver	X_1	X_1	X_2	X_1	X_1	X_1	X_1	X_1	
		supply reliability	X_1	X_1	X_2	X_1	X_1	X_1	X_1	X_1	
		acceptance of delivery					X_2	X_2	X_2	X_1	
		order volume reliability		X_2	X_2	X_2	X_2	X_2	X_2	X_1	
		supply quality guarantee	X_2	X_2	X_1	X_1	X_1	X_1	X_1	X_1	
		acceptance tolerance		X_2	X_2	X_2				X_2	
	customer service policies	production-specific adjustment		X_2	X_2	X_1	X_1	X_1	X_1	X_1	
		sales-specific adjustments					X_2	X_2	X_2		
		assembly / develop / testing	X_1								
		maintenance / repairs / service	X_1			X_2	X_2	X_2	X_2		
		provision of spare parts	X_1			X_1	X_1	X_1	X_1		
		staff support	X_2				X_2	X_2	X_2		
		materials provisioning					X_2	X_2	X_2		
		after-sales service				X_2	X_2	X_2	X_2		
		recycling service		X_2	X_2	X_1	X_1	X_1	X_1	X_1	
	guarantee policies	scope of guarantee	X_2			X_2	X_1	X_1	X_1		
		guarantee period	X_2			X_2	X_1	X_1	X_1		
		guarantee performance	X_2			X_2	X_1	X_1	X_1		
		goodwill	X_1	X_2	X_2	X_2	X_1	X_1	X_1	X_2	
	performance assurance policies	quality audits	X_2	X_2	X_2	X_1	X_1	X_1	X_1	X_1	
		quality documentation				X_1	X_1	X_1	X_1		
		TQM	X_2	X_2	X_2	X_1	X_1	X_1	X_1	X_1	
		schedule control	X_1	X_2	X_2	X_2	X_2	X_2	X_2	X_1	

Illustration 61: Hierarchy of procurement instruments for service policies

(3) Suitability of procurement instruments for supply policies

Illustration 62 shows procurement instruments for supply policies in an hierarchical order.

tool variables and tool variable effects			singular product	cheap product	standard product	established product	top product	innovative product	purchaser-specific product	quantity significance	etc.
Supply policy	supply quantity policies	small order quantity	X_1						X_2	X_2	
		large order quantity		X_1	X_2					X_1	
		variable order quantity				X_2	X_2	X_2	X_2		
		exact order quantity		X_1	X_1	X_1	X_1	X_1	X_1	X_1	
	procurement organisation policies	centralized purchasing	X_1	X_2	X_2	X_1	X_1	X_1	X_1	X_1	
		decentralized purchasing	X_2	X_2	X_2	X_1	X_2	X_2	X_2	X_2	
		purchasing offices		X_2	X_2	X_1				X_2	
		local puchasers		X_2	X_2	X_1				X_2	
		purchasing agents		X_2	X_2	X_1				X_2	
		purchasing cooperation		X_2		X_1				X_1	
	supply contract policies	waste management		X_2	X_2	X_1		X_1	X_1	X_1	
		framework agreement		X_2	X_2	X_1	X_1	X_1	X_1	X_1	
		subcontracting	X_2				X_2	X_2	X_2		
		consignment stock				X_2	X_2	X_2	X_2		
		exclusive rights				X_2	X_2	X_2	X_1		
		capacity booking				X_2	X_2	X_2	X_1	X_2	
		fixed deals	X_2	X_2		X_3	X_3	X_3	X_3	X_2	
		ex-works terms		X_2	X_2	X_2	X_2	X_2	X_2	X_3	
		carrier acceptance terms	X_2	X_2	X_2	X_2	X_2	X_2	X_2	X_2	
		cost acceptance terms	X_2	X_2	X_2	X_2	X_2	X_2	X_2	X_1	
		destination acceptance terms	X_1	X_1	X_2	X_2	X_2	X_2	X_2	X_1	
		recycling of materials		X_2	X_2	X_1	X_1	X_1	X_1	X_1	
	logistical policies	central storage facilities		X_2	X_2	X_2	X_2	X_2	X_2	X_2	
		decentralized storage facilities	X_1	X_2	X_2	X_2	X_2	X_2	X_2	X_2	
		external storage facilities		X_2	X_2	X_2	X_2	X_2	X_2	X_2	
		stipulated means of transport					X_2	X_2	X_2		
		stipulated carrier		X_2	X_2	X_2	X_1	X_1	X_1	X_2	
		stipulated routes of transport		X_2		X_2				X_2	
		stipulated means of communication	X_2	X_2	X_2	X_2	X_1	X_1	X_1	X_1	

Illustration 62: Hierarchy of procurement instruments for supply policies

It is obvious that major importance is given to order quantities. Centralized purchasing departments seem to be more popular than decentralized purchasing offices. Tool

124

variable effects such as purchasing offices abroad, purchasing trips, purchasing agents and purchasing consortiums which are typical for international purchasing operations are also quite common in companies which order large quantities. Cooperation in the field of waste disposal and recycling seems to be a procurement instrument which is generally accepted. The same applies to the negotiation of framework agreements. The use of the Incoterms varies considerably in different lines of business. Fixed deals seem to be more common in the trade sector than in the industrial sector which is the reason why it is classified as being of rather low importance here. Logistical issues seem to be widely considered as quite important, but not critical.

(4) Suitability of procurement instruments for remuneration policies
Illustration 63 shows procurement instruments for remuneration policies in an hierarchical order.

Apart from terms of payment policies, which vary considerably in different lines of business, views on these procurement instruments differ greatly. Exerting price pressure seems particularly popular in companies which order large quantities at low target prices; attractive prices are only offered where high performance products are purchased. Purchasers which have a target costing approach are naturally interested in target prices. Price acceptance, performance-related prices and fixed prices seem suitable when high performance products are purchased, while competition-related prices are more common in companies which purchase low performance products. Both options seem to be applied with varying intensity when singular products are purchased.

		tool variables and tool variable effects / object characteristics	singular product	cheap product	standard product	established product	top product	innovative product	purchaser-specific product	quantity significance	etc.
Remuneration policiy	price policies	price pressure		X_1	X_2	X_2				X_1	
		attractive prices					X_1	X_1	X_1		
		target prices	X_2	X_1	X_2	X_1	X_2	X_2	X_1	X_1	
		price acceptance	X_2				X_1	X_1	X_2		
		performance-related prices	X_1				X_1	X_1	X_1		
		competition-related prices	X_1	X_1	X_1	X_2				X_1	
		fixed prices	X_2			X_1	X_2	X_3	X_2		
		price adjustments	X_2	X_2		X_2	X_2	X_2	X_2	X_2	
	discount policies	quantity discount			X_1	X_2				X_1	
		first order / regular order		X_2	X_3	X_2		X_3	X_3	X_2	
		special service discount				X_2	X_3	X_2	X_3	X_2	
		cash discount	X_2	X_2	X_2	X_2	X_2	X_2	X_2	X_2	
		no additional charges for small order volumens						X_2	X_2		
	bonus policies	priority bonus	X_2	X_2		X_2	X_1	X_1	X_2	X_2	
		quantity bonus			X_2	X_2				X_1	
		time bonus	X_1				X_2	X_2	X_2		
		special service bonus					X_2	X_2	X_1		
	penalty policies		X_1	X_2		X_2	X_2	X_2	X_1	X_2	
	payment terms policies	payment institutions	X_2	X_2	X_2	X_2	X_2	X_2	X_2	X_2	
		payment modus	X_2	X_2	X_2	X_2	X_2	X_2	X_2	X_2	
		payment schedule	X_2	X_2	X_2	X_2	X_2	X_2	X_2	X_2	
		payment currency	X_2	X_2	X_2	X_2	X_2	X_2	X_2	X_2	
		payment guarantee	X_2	X_2	X_2	X_2	X_2	X_2	X_2	X_2	
	credit policies	supplier credit allowance	X_1			X_2	X_2	X_1	X_1	X_2	
		supplier credit request	X_2				X_2	X_2	X_2		
		capital investment				X_3	X_3	X_3	X_3		

Illustration 63: Hierarchy of procurement instruments of remuneration policies

The variety of discount policies is still more elaborately used in the trade sector than in the industrial sector, with the only exception being the payment of cash discounts. The more valuable the products are, the less common it seems to "haggle" for discounts. Performance bonuses are quite common where high performance products are purchased, however, quantity discounts are, not surprisingly, only given when large orders are placed. Penalty policies are applied when specific products are critical for production planning and scheduling, especially when buying plants (machines) or purchaser-specific products. Allowing or asking for financial loans and credits is only common when object performance characteristics are significant.

(5) Suitability of procurement instruments for communication policies

Illustration 64 shows that almost all procurement instruments are suitable for special procurement object characteristics. When standard products are purchased special communication instruments do not seem necessary.

Communication policy	tool variables	object characteristics →	singular product	cheap product	standard product	established product	top product	innovative product	purchaser-specific product	quantity significance	etc.
	contact policies	openness	X_2	X_1		X_1	X_1	X_1	X_1	X_1	
		competence	X_2	X_2		X_2	X_1	X_1	X_1	X_1	
		suitable media	X_2	X_1		X_1	X_1	X_1	X_1	X_1	
		buyer's trade fair		X_1	X_2	X_1				X_1	
		supplier discussion day				X_2	X_2	X_1	X_2	X_1	
	procurement process handling	offer handling	X_2	X_1	X_2	X_2	X_1	X_1	X_1	X_1	
		feedback to rejected offers	X_3		X_2	X_2	X_2	X_1	X_1		
		ordering and cancellation	X_2	X_1	X_2	X_2	X_2	X_2	X_2	X_1	
		invoicing		X_2	X_2	X_2	X_2	X_2	X_2	X_1	
		complaints and disputes	X_2	X_2	X_2	X_2	X_2	X_2	X_2	X_1	
	know-how transfer policies	communicate problems	X_1				X_2	X_1	X_1		
		confidentiality					X_1	X_1	X_1		
		market information					X_2	X_2	X_1	X_2	
		product application advise	X_1				X_1	X_1	X_1		
		consulting services					X_2	X_2	X_3	X_3	X_2
	reference policies	supplier's references	X_1				X_1	X_1	X_1	X_1	
		purchaser's references					X_3	X_2	X_2	X_1	X_2
		third party references					X_3	X_3	X_3		
	advertising policies	supplier competitions					X_2	X_2	X_2	X_3	X_1
		advertising of demands					X_2	X_2	X_2	X_1	X_2
		direct advertising					X_1	X_1	X_2		

Illustration 64: Hierarchy of procurement instruments for communication policies

(6) Checking the overall matrix

After having combined procurement object characteristics (e.g. top product with high significance of quantity) specifically, suitable procurement instruments can be selected. You have to check whether the recommended procurement instruments are actually suitable in a specific demand situation. This systematical approach can be translated into a comprehensive catalogue of questions. Any alterations and amendments can be explained in detail here, thus creating a transparent protocol for later reference in similar decision-making situations. This protocol should include the targeted costs of applying incentive-oriented procurement instruments. Although these costs can only be rough estimates, they are nevertheless important to support cost-performance thinking and facilitate future calculations. When considering possible incentives, the competition issue always has to be taken into consideration as well. Illustration 65 shows the market power portfolio, illustrating situations you could be confronted with in procurement.

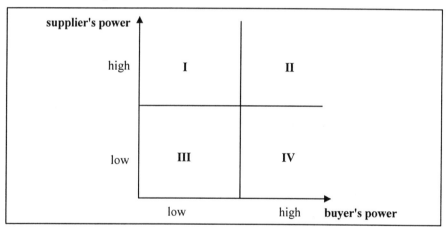

Illustration 65: Market power portfolio

It is quite obvious that the purchaser has to offer more incentives in Situation I than in Situation IV. In negotiations between equal partners win-win strategies should be applied to secure satisfactory results for all partners involved.

4.53 The Negotiating Process

Illustration 66 shows a typical purchasing negotiation process.

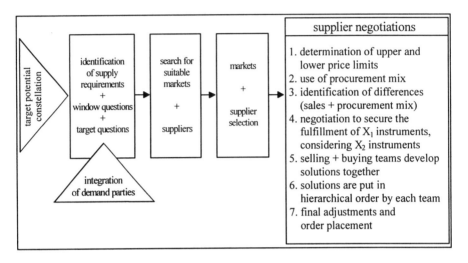

Illustration 66: The purchasing negotiation process

The first stages of situation analysis (constellations, potentials and targets) up to the selection of potential suppliers have already been described in detail. Now we want to look into possible approaches for the negotiating process itself. In accordance with the coalition and the incentive-contribution theory we want partnership and cooperation to be the basis for negotiation processes in procurement.

A possible scenario could be as follows:

Following your company's target costing approach you have calculated the maximum possible cost of a procurement object (see Hiromoto 1989, p. 320), thus identifying your upper price limit. In a comprehensive purchase cost analysis you have calculated as well what the minimum cost of the procurement object under optimum production conditions would be, thus establishing your lower price limit. Prior to the negotiation you let your supplier know this lower price limit and use some selected procurement instruments which suit the respective procurement object characteristics. In combination with a detailed description of the procurement object this provides the supplier with important information for the negotiation process. He can now clearify which of the purchaser's supply requirements his company can meet and then come to the negotiation prepared and with concrete ideas and solutions. It is particularly important to give the supplier a chance to check with his company which of the purchaser's incentives are of interest and relevance to him. As the purchaser normally has only limited knowledge of the supplier's situation, the supplier has to provide the necessary information on his current targets and production planning.

In a first round of negotiations between purchaser and supplier all points they agree or disagree upon are known and can be discussed. Depending on how critical the disagreements are, it can be useful to organize meetings between purchasing and selling teams, giving them the task to look for solutions which are mutually satisfactory. Such discussions might reveal, e.g., that adjustments in the production process of the supplier could lead to considerable cost reductions provided that the order volume of the procurement object is increased. In this case the purchasing team can see whether this particular procurement object could be standardized for use in other products of their range . And once it has been established that such a step would not cause additional costs for the purchaser, a viable solutions can be reached between the parties.

This example illustrates how a network approach can help to identify optimum solutions for procurement problems.

Every party in a negotiation has its own priorities which are reflected in their fixed tartgets. However, they are also strongly influenced by the personalities of the negotiators. In order to increase the consensus within the group it might be a useful to suggest that both the purchasing and the selling team put the suggested solutions in a hierachical order. Especially when the people involved have not dealt with each other before such an approach might help to overcome obstacles in the negotiating process. After having established an overall negotiating solution, however, this intermediate step can be abandoned and the negotiators can concentrate straight away on identifying comprehensive solutions.

4.6 Procurement Process Handling

Operative planning tasks prevail in the handling of procurement processes while the strategical part is quite limited

Materials planning and scheduling is one of the most important parts of procurement (materials management). In view of an increasing number of problems between internal and external functions in the corporate added value chain, it might be worth a thought to integrate materials planning and scheduling in the logistics function and to merge it with production control. Once this has been done, materials planning and scheduling is in charge of the physical movement of goods whereas planning and optimizing processes are centralized. Such a materials planning and scheduling function could also take over quality management responsibilities. Like logistics, quality management is an interface function coordinating activities in different corporate functions.

4.61 Orders

(1) Orders are the formal conclusion of a supply decision reached between purchaser and supplier. The conclusion of a contract creates a relationship of debenture between purchaser and supplier.

An order states the purchaser's commitment that he or a third party will accept, at the conditions stated in the order, the goods described in the order upon delivery from either the supplier or a named subsupplier. Orders can be based on existing contracts (e.g. delivery on call), they can express acceptance of a contract, or they can be an application to conclude a contract. If an order is placed in acceptance of a firm offer, a contract is concluded between purchaser and supplier as soon as the supplier receives the formal order. If an order is placed based on an offer without obligation, an order confirmation on part of the supplier is required for the conclusion of a contract. An order is merely an application for the conclusion of contract, however, if it is not based on a formal offer or if it differs from the offer submitted by the supplier. In these cases the formal conclusion of contract requires a confirmation on part of the supplier as well. In some countries like, e.g. Germany, business parners can conclude contracts on the basis of "silence means acceptance" as well (see Kopsidis 1992, p. 99).

(2) In business practice there are standard agreements and special agreements. Long negotiations and incentive-request strategies do not tend to be viable when procurement objects are purchased in smaller quantities or are not critical for production. Standard contracts are concluded in these cases. The more procurement instruments are being used and the more comprehensive procurement strategies are to be realized, however, the more important special contracts and agreements between the contractual parties become. Although German law, for example, allows freedom of contract, it still has to be established what kind of implications and legal consequences a contract might have. When engaging in international procurement and global sourcing strategies, knowledge of national laws and regulations does not suffice. For that kind of operations a purchaser requires a thorough knowledge of the possibilities and limitations created through international laws and regulations. For standard procurement operations there are some internationally accepted standards such as the Incoterms. For better transparency and understanding of contractual obligations you should always try and stipulate that the place of jurisdiction shall be in your country and that the contract shall be subject to the laws of your country.

You can look at contracts from a legal and supply technical point of view as well. Supply contracts in Germany, for example, are based on the German law of contract as stipulated in German BGB law. There are

– sales contracts (§§ 433)
– contracts for work (§§ 631) and contracts for service
– tenancy agreements
– leasing agreements
– rental agreements

Other types of contracts (e.g. loan agreements) have not been included in this list as they are of no relevance for the procurement objects we are examining here.

Supply-technical types of contracts such as framework agreements with suppliers have a supply focus. We have already discussed a variety of contracts used by purchasers in chapter 3.523.

(3) An order recaps the result of a negotiation process and reflects

- the power of the negotiating partners,
- the targets of the negotiating partners,
- any incentive-request tactics and strategies applied in the negotiation.

The negotiating process can lead to considerable modifications of initial supply requirements, with the target being to optimize the respective deal for all parties involved. The statements made here are therefore more abstract than in Illustration 35. An order has to include information on the following issues:

- quantity,
- required performance levels,
- time of delivery,
- place of delivery,
- terms of delivery,
- price,
- service,
- other information.

It is not necessary to include in an order information about the procurement instruments applied as these are merely the means for reaching an agreement, the end product of which the order is.

4.62 Order Fulfillment Control

Order fulfillment control is another function for which logistics could take responsibility.

After having stipulated in the contract which performances (quality and quantity of product, service, performance levels, information) have to be fulfilled at what cost where and when, it is necessary to make sure that the contractual obligations are actually fulfilled. This type of procurement control is a process which ensures the fulfillment of a contract.

(1) Total Quality Management is a central issue when monitoring performances. Special process and object related steps have to be taken to ensure that no errors or mistakes occur in production so and performance deficiencies have to be dealt with later. Thus supply security is increased and procurement costs are reduced. Ensuring that a procurement object meets required performance level is a comprehensive task which has to be fulfilled by purchaser and supplier together. This task is by no means limited to warehouse controls on part of the supplier or incoming goods inspection on part of the purchaser (see Berndt 1995).

(2) The most intensive kind of quantity control is realized where just-in-time strategies have been implemented. In some lines of business (e.g. the automotive industry) where parts and components have to be delivered directly to the assembly line at exact intervalls, it is simply not acceptable that problems should arise regarding quantities, delivery schedules or locations. It is essential to coordiante production and delivery schedules in detail. This can be done by using integrated production, planning and controlling systems.

(3) A major part of modality control is realized through incoming goods inspection and the relevant data collected there. This is a point where the request to use suitable information technology is particularly important. Companies which still exchange information traditionally by mailing order forms in duplicate and triplicate will find it difficult to survive in a competitive marketplace where time and flexibility are critical factors. It is necessary to implement suitable systems and programmes (e-mail, internet, EDI) which allow paperless, simultaneous exchange of data. The implementation of such technology makes continuous invoice controls through the purchasing departments redundant. Only in case of discrepancies between invoices received and goods delivered is the purchaser in charge informed automatically.

4.63 Recycling and Waste Disposal

Illustration 67 demonstrates that the procurement function is not only resonsible for the provisioning of services and supplies but also for waste disposal and recycling. Any materials which are not used up by the company in the production process can re-enter the economic circle.

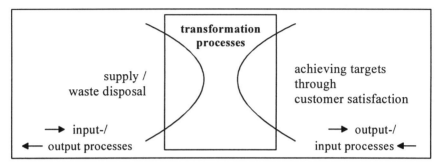

Illustration 67: Transformation processes

If you know your supply markets and suppliers, you will also know how to handle recycling materials economically, i.e. how to recycle or dispose of waste at minimum costs or, respecitively, optimum profits.

According to Illustration 67 you can input corporate transformation processes in a way which produces output for covering the demand of third parties. The transformation of standard input such as production material might lead to materials being left over; other materials might be damaged in production and end up as waste or scrap; after years of usage investment goods, machines and tools have to be replaced. Procurement objects on stock can become obsolete when a company redesigns or updates its products. Due to more strict environmental regulations in the future companies might increasingly have to allow their customers to return end products for recycling and waste disposal. Part of the objects which have to be disposed of can be recycled, i.e. reintroduced in the supply process for either your own company or third parties. The other objects have to be destroyed and disposed of. This still accounts for the major part of corporate waste disposal management today. Illustration 68 shows waste disposal as a circular process.

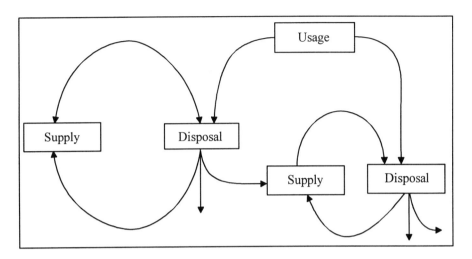

Illustration 68: Waste disposal as a circular process

As shown in Illustration 69, waste disposal management has several aspects, some of which are of major interest for the procurement function.

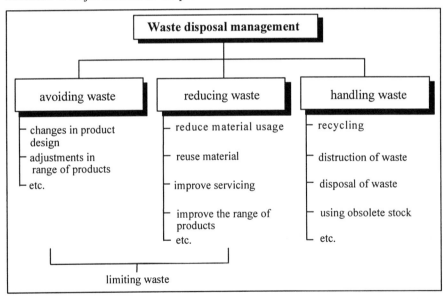

Illustration 69: Waste disposal management

Waste disposal deals with the problem of handling waste. There are different possibilities if you have to dispose of waste:

– Recycling material means to process waste or scrap material either internally or externally (e.g. use fish bones for producing fish meal); or you can recycle materials (e.g. recycling paper, scrap); or you can reuse materials (e.g. conversion and adaptation of old units and components) or you can use materials for another purpose (e.g. use old polishing cloths as cleaning cloths).

– When destroying material chemically, thermically or biologically sophisticated methods and processes can be used to change the substance of the material to be destroyed. These processes can generate waste again (e.g. slag, clinker or mud) which has to be disposed of.

– In most cases waste is disposed of by simply having it taken to a tip.

– The disposal of obsolete inventories is a special case which can call for any of the above mentioned solutions. The most viable solution, however, would be to return the unused materials to the supplier who might be able to resell them. This tends to be an easy solution as far as customer and standard goods are concerned, but with purchaser-specific objects you might not have such an option.

Waste can be disposed of in a way that is

– cost intensive,
– profitable,
– does not generate neither costs nor profits.

The destruction of waste tends to be cost intensive. In the future companies will increasingly be forced to pay high fees and charges for the distruction and disposal of waste. It will be more difficult to shift the cost responsibility for waste generated internally. Trying to avoid and reduce waste in your production and searching for viable recycling and reusage possibilities will therefore become a critical issue in the future.

Waste recycling and reusage can be handled

– in-house,
– in cooperation with other companies,
– by third parties.

Decisions on that subject usually depend on the risks and costs involved as well as the profits that might be generated in the process. The higher the risk, the more we recommend to leave this task to external specialists who have the necessary knowledge of existing laws and can make sure that relevant regulations are observed. When considering possible costs and profits in the process do not forget to calculate handling and management costs. Design a procurement instrument mix with both requests and incentives for your supplier, thus securing optimum results for your company.

4.7 Information / Control

Prior to making a decision information has to be gathered. As this process generates costs it is important to apply the economic principle and try to gather relevant information at the lowest possible cost. However, it is not only difficult to anticipate the cost of collecting data, but to decide which information is required in the first place. Information can essentially be obtained internally (procurement control) and externally (supply market research).

4.71 Supply Market Research

Supply market research differs from sales market research in some vital points:
- Sales market research usually focuses on anonymous mass markets. In supply market research, on the other hand, there is a limited number of suppliers which have to be examined in order to identify the best possible supplier for a company. The focus is therefore on singular relationships.
- In sales market research the number of products researched at a time tends to be small. Complexity increases with production. As opposed to that, the number of materials, parts and components which a company has to purchase is much higher and causes considerable selection problems.
- Sales market research, especially in consumer goods markets, focuses strongly on emotional and irrational responses of potential customers to the products in question. Supply market research concentrates on de facto requirements.

138

These differences lead to different approaches in supply and sales market research. Illustration 70 shows the overall structure of supply market research.

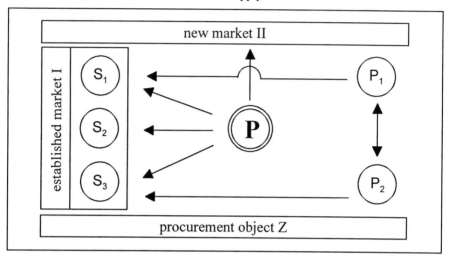

Illustration 70: Supply market research

As a rule, the purchaser (P) contacts the supplier (S1 - S3) in an established market. He is interested in the scope of supply and services provided by the supplier, about his costs and the intensity of competition in the supply market. As he is not likely to be the only purchaser in the market, he requires information about his buying competitors in the market as well (P1-P3). The purchaser has to be able to assess and anticipate the competition he might be faced with in a supply market if he wants to use his incentive-contribution instruments and strategies successfully in a negotiation.

Apart from operating in established markets, new markets have to be examined for future business. If your established markets are highly developed and offer state-of-the-art products, your target will hardly be to look for technological developments and new technical solutions but for cost saving potentials and higher flexibility. However, after having preselected a number of suppliers, you have to check their performance levels as well. In that situation the purchaser requires comprehensive information on suppliers, markets and buying competitors in the market.

Stangle (1985) suggested the following approach for supply market research:

1. select which procurement objects you want to focus on;

2. define which information is relevant for the procurement of these objects;

3. gather the relevant information;

4. analyse the relevant information you have collected.

This economical approach helps to prevent mountains of unnecessary information.

4.711 Selecting Procurement Objects for Supply Market Research

Which procurement objects are worth engaging in supply market research? The research of which procurement object is likely to generate the biggest profits? This question is the more important, the more limited your internal capacities are.

Let us have another look at the selection criteria we discussed in chapter 4.21. Provided that there is time at all for supply market research in daily buisness, ABC analyses seem the most common way to decide which procurement objects are worth special research.

This situation, however, is not satisfactory. Consider the following case: a company has been fighting for some time to improve the sales quality of its products (performance consistency). However, there have been repeated performance problems caused by a bought-out part in the value of not more than DM 2.30. Is this viable? Here´s another situation: for the purchaser of a gas supply company the costs of the turbines required for gas pipelines may not be critical, even though they might be well worth half a million German marks each. Are these procurement objects still worth special market research activities?

The approaches commonly applied so far have not proved to be sufficient. For a more sophisticated approach we can look at a number of important criteria and relate them to the basic procurement targets we discussed before. Possible criteria could be

- cost significance,

- performance significance,

- security significance,

- flexibility significance.

Cost significance means that the procurement object has a strong influence on the total cost of the primary object (end product). This could be a singular object when only this one object has to be incorporated or processed; or it could be several objects. The significance of the latter can be established mathematically by multiplying quantity and price. Thus cost significance is the counterpart of the procurement object characteristic "price significance".

Performance significance indicates the influence of the procurement object on the performance of the end product (see procurement object characteristic "performance significance" described in chapter 2.24). Products which are critical for the performance of the end product do not necessarily have to be expensive. They can either have a high level of performance or have a long life and high performance consistency.

Security significance indicates a high level of security regarding order quantities and schedules. If the sale of a product is prone to extreme seasonal fluctuations (e.g. fashion products or sweets), schedules and quantities are of considerable significance because the value of the products fluctuates as well.

Flexibility significance is mainly an issue when procurement objects are accessories for a complete product (e.g. cars and furniture). In that case it depends entirely on the end customer which parts he will order. When short delivery times are used as an instrument for securing orders (time between order and delivery is to be reduced), flexibility becomes a major issue. This can mean both flexibility regarding quantities as well as performance levels (flexibility regarding product types and qualities).

We want to select procurement objects against the background of specific procurement situations and include procurement object characteristics (if-conditions) into our considerations as well.

Illustration 71 may help to select procurement objects with a view to a certain target.

procurement product targets / functional procurement targets	singular product	cheap product	standard product	established product	top product	innovative product	purchaser-specific product	significance of quantity	etc.
cost reduction		X		X				X	
increase in performance	X				X	X	X		
risk reduction				X	X	X	X	X	
increase in flexibility				X	X	X	X		

Illustration 71: Targeted selection of procurement objects

The illustration shows that procurement activities with a special view to "cost signifi-cance" focus on the procurement object characteristics cheap product, established product and high importance of quantities. That means that. these procurement objects are suitable for supply market research activities if your main target is to reduce costs. When the target "performance significance" prevails, the illustration shows singular products, state-of-the-art products, innovative products and top products. When "secu-rity significance" defines procurement targets the illustration shows established prod-ucts, top products, innovative and special products as well as a high importance of quantities. Where "flexibility significance" is the most important criterion, we can concentrate on established products, top products, innovative and special products. Furthermore, the illustration shows that

– with some procurement objects different targets justify supply market research;

– some procurement objects can be allocated clearly to one procurement target;

– standard products do not seem worth special supply market evaluations.

After these considerations we can go back to Illustration 31 and specify the importance of supply market research activities:

If you look into the criteria "cost significance", "performance significance" etc and establish that a new procurement object belongs to category B or C, it does not seem neither viable or even necessary to engage in any supply market research activities for the time being.

142

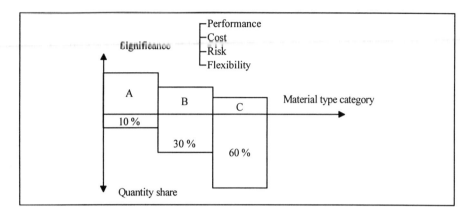

Illustration 72: Assessment of material types based on the criterion performance significance

4.712 Procurement Information

The next step is to decide which information is of interest in a specific demand situation. Illustration 73 shows the main information blocks in supply market research.

buyer	supplier
requirements ⟶	performance information
performances ⟶	requirements information
information about buyer's competitors	information about supplier's competitors
General information about markets	

Illustration 73: Information blocks in supply market research

Due to the strategical approach we have chosen in procurement marketing there are more areas of information to be looked into than in traditional market research (see Arnold, 1995, and others).

(1) Performance information: Which information on your supplier's performances you require depends entirely on your company's actual supply requirements. It is not necessary to look for information that is not relevant for a specific demand situation. We can therefore modify Illustration 35 by replacing requirements with information (see Illustration 74).

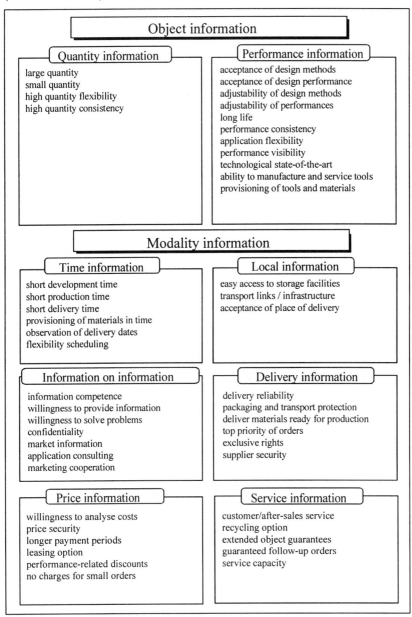

Illustration 74: Performance information

144

(2) Requirement information: In accordance with the incentive-contribution theory which we have chosen as the basis for strategical supply decisions we require information on what our suppliers want, what kind of problems they might have and what might be particularly interesting for them. When entering into negotiations with a supplier we need to know what might be of interest to him. The challenge for the purchaser is to achieve the best price for his company by offering his supplier incentives which are not too cost-intensive. The more the purchaser knows about the needs and demands of his suppliers, the more effectively can he use his set of procurement instruments. Illustration 75 shows demands which are important from the supplier's point of view.

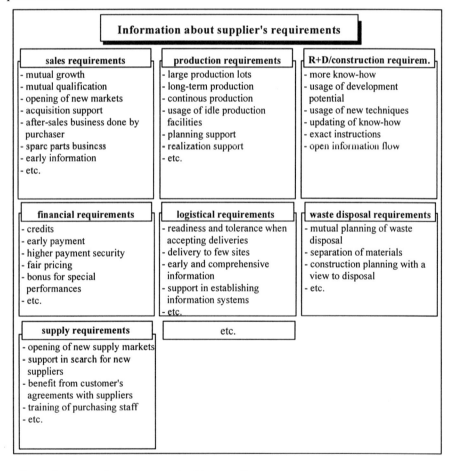

Illustration 75: Information required by suppliers

The structure shown here illustrates how functions need to overcome their traditional boundaries and start to network. Everyday procurement business is currently at a stage where any question in that direction is likely to raise eyebrows. It is still the exception that purchasers should actually seek to look at a deal from their supplier's point of view. The more the optimization of the entire added value chain comes into focus, the more important this approach will be.

(3) Information on supplier's competitors: Purchasers do not only require information on the performances of individual suppliers, they also need to be able to compare their suppliers' performances in their respective markets. Traditional market research defines the terms polypolistic, oligopolistic and monopolistic supply structures. These depend on

– product competition,

– sales terms,

– future innovations,

– the number of competitors and the fierceness of competition in a market.

Product competition and sales terms can be summarized under the aspect performance competition. All relevant data can be gathered from the supplier's up-to-date performance information. This information, however, is static and does not give any information about a supplier's future potentials and performances. Therefore it is interesting to look into his potential for future innovations. Which supplier is currently increasing or decreasing which capacities? From this information you can deduct the intensity of competition in the respective market.

(4) Information on purchaser's competitors: It is essential to identify possible competition on the buying side by using, e.g., the matrix shown in Illustration 76.

Input \ Output	same end product	different end product
same procurement object	1	2
same material	3	4
same process	5	6

Illustration 76: Identifying potential buying competitors

The easiest way is to start with your competitors on the sales side. It is very likely that these competitors require at least similar procurement objects like you (see Field 1 in the matrix). If you and your competitors require the same materials for the same kind of end product you are likely to have to deal with cyclical demand fluctuations (e.g., bull and bear trends in steel prices).

Field 5 in the matrix indicates a lower level of competition. This is the case when the same process or material is offered by many sources. Fields 2 and 4 are more critical, however. If you require a certain material for several of your end products, you have to observe different demand cycles. When the same material is used in different lines of business and their demand cycles happen to experience the same fluctuations at the same time, you should not be surprised about sometimes rather extreme price fluctuations.

Field 6 represents the most difficult part of the matrix because you need to identify your competitors first before you can assess the processes and approaches they apply. If, e.g., company A conducts a purchase price analysis and consequently forces his supplier to reduce his prices for him by 20%, company B, which does not negotiate such a price reduction, runs the risk of unknowingly having to compensate for his supplier´s losses. This applies to all aspects which require decisions:

– selection of procurement instruments,
– selection of markets and suppliers,
– selection of targets and strategies,
– selection of methods to be applied.

Furthermore, it has to be established how important a competitor is in the market.

Which parts are bought in large quantities? What procurement potentials do I have to expect on part of the supplier (see chapter 4.13)?

(5) Market information: Here we can take another look at the characteristics of market analyses as described in chapter 4.31. The characteristsics shown in Illustration 40 equal the market information required.

4.713 Selection of Information

For the selection of relevant information we have to refer to procurement object characteristics (if-conditions) again. Which information is important for a decision in a given situation and which is not depends entirely on the circumstances of the situation as well as the required procurement object characteristics. We shall focus on how to identify relevant information for a decision here.

(1) For selecting relevant performance information let us refer to Illustration 36 again in which we established which supply requirements are important for which procurement object characteristics. This matrix can be adapted for the present context with only minor adjustments. Thus less efforts are required when programming the computer-aided decision support system we recommended earlier. Illustration 77 shows an adjusted matrix for the selection of relevant performance information.

Information about supplier performances		singular product	cheap product	standard product	established product	top product	innovative product	purchaser-specific product	significance of quantity	etc.
quantity information	large quantity		X_1	X_1	X_2				X_1	
	small quantity	X_1				X_2	X_2	X_2		
	high significance of quantity			X_2					X_2	
	high quantity consistency					X_1	X_1	X_1	X_1	
performance information	acceptance of design methods	X_1				X_1	X_1	X_1		
	acceptance of design performances	X_1				X_1	X_1	X_1		
	adjustability of design methods						X_2			
	adjustability of performances					X_1	X_1	X_1	X_2	
	long life	X_2				X_1	X_2	X_2		
	performance consistency			X_1	X_1				X_1	
	application flexibility		X_2	X_1						
	visibility of performance					X_1	X_1			
	technological state-of-the-art	X_1				X_1	X_1	X_1		
	ability to manufacture tools	X_2					X_2	X_2		
	provisioning of tools and materials				X_2				X_3	
time information	short development time					X_2	X_1	X_1		
	short production time		X_1		X_2				X_1	
	short delivery time		X_1	X_1	X_2				X_1	
	provisioning of materials in time			X_1	X_1				X_1	
	observation of delivery data	X_2	X_1	X_1	X_1				X_1	
	flexible scheduling			X_2	X_2					
location information	easy access to storage facilities			X_3	X_2				X_2	
	transport links / infrastructure			X_2	X_2				X_2	
	acceptance of place of delivery			X_2	X_2	X_2			X_2	
delivery information	supplier reliability		X_1	X_2	X_1	X_1	X_1	X_1	X_1	
	packaging and transport protection	X_2				X_2	X_2	X_2		
	deliver materials ready for production		X_1	X_1	X_2				X_1	
	top priority of orders					X_2	X_2	X_1		
	exclusive rights					X_2	X_2	X_1		
	supplier security	X_1			X_1	X_1	X_1	X_1	X_1	
price information	willingness to analyse costs	X_1			X_1	X_2	X_2		X_1	
	price security	X_2			X_2				X_2	
	longer payment periods	X_2						X_3		
	leasing option	X_2								
	performance-related discount				X_2				X_2	
	no charges for small orders			X_2	X_2					
Service information	after-sales-service	X_1			X_1	X_1	X_1			
	recycling option	X_2	X_1	X_2	X_2	X_2	X_2	X_2	X_1	
	extended object guarantee	X_1			X_2					
	guaranteed follow-up orders				X_1					
	service capacity	X_3				X_3	X_3	X_3		
Information about information	information competence	X_2				X_1	X_1	X_1		
	willingness to provide information	X_2				X_1	X_1	X_1		
	willingness to solve problems	X_1				X_1	X_1	X_1		
	confidentiality					X_2	X_2	X_1		
	market information					X_2	X_2	X_2		
	application consulting	X_2				X_2	X_2	X_2		
	marketing cooperation					X_2	X_2			

Illustration 77: Selecting performance information

(2) We can choose a similar approach for the selection of *supply requirement information*. The matrix shown in Illustration 78 is based on Illustration 47.

Information about supplier requirements	conditions (object characteristics)	singular product	cheap product	standard product	established product	top product	innovative product	purchaser-specific product	quantity significance	etc.
sales requirements	mutual growth				X	X	X	X	X	
	mutual qualification	X			X	X	X	X		
	opening of new markets					X	X			
	aquisition support	X				X	X		X	
	spare parts business				X	X	X	X		
	after-sales business done by purchaser				X	X	X	X		
	early information					X	X	X		
	etc.									
R+D/construction requirements	more know-how	X				X		X		
	usage of development potential	X				X	X	X		
	usage of new techniques	X				X	X	X		
	updating of know-how					X	X	X		
	exact instructions	X			X	X		X	X	
	open information flow	X				X	X	X		
	etc.									
production requirements	large production lots		X	X	X				X	
	long-term production		X	X	X		X	X	X	
	continous production		X	X	X	X	X	X	X	
	usage of idle production facilities		X	X				X	X	
	planning support	X			X	X		X	X	
	realization support	X			X	X		X	X	
	etc.									
supply requirements	opening of new supply markets		X	X				X	X	
	support in search for new suppliers		X	X	X	X		X	X	
	benefit from customers agreements withs.		X	X	X	X		X	X	
	training of purchasing stuff					X	X	X		
	etc.									
financial requirements	credits	X				X	X	X		
	early payment	X	X	X	X	X	X	X	X	
	higher payment security	X	X	X	X	X	X	X	X	
	fair pricing	X			X	X	X	X	X	
	bonus for special performances	X				X		X		
	etc.									
logistical requirements	readiness and tolerance when accepting deliveries		X	X	X			X	X	
	delivery to few places		X	X	X				X	
	early and comprehensive information	X			X	X	X	X		
	support in establishing information system					X	X	X		
	etc.									
waste disposal req.	mutual planning of waste disposal		X		X	X	X	X	X	
	separation of materials		X		X	X	X	X	X	
	construction planning witha view to waste disposal				X	X	X	X		
	etc.									

Illustration 78: Selecting requirement information

The illustrated requirement information can be used effectively in supplier negotiations. It should suffice to work out which supply requirements are important for the characteristics of the procurement object in question and select suitable incentive instruments accordingly.

(3) *Information on your supplier's competitors* tends to be less specific and cannot really be linked direcly to procurement object characteristics. This information has to be gathered on a general level and kept up-to-date.

(4) *Market information* again is more specific. Therefore we can modify Illustration 47 as shown in Illustration 79.

conditions (object characteristics) / Information about markets	singular product	cheap product	standard product	established product	top produt	innovative product	purchaser-specific product	significance of quantity	etc.
performances work performance	X_1			X_2	X_1	X_1	X_1	X_2	
management performance	X_1				X_1	X_1	X_1	X_2	
technology	X_1				X_1	X_1	X_1		
logistics performance		X_1	X_1					X_1	
communication performance	X_1				X_1	X_1	X_1		
capital performance			X_2	X_2				X_2	
national economics			X_2	X_2		X_3	X_3		
costs labour costs	X_2	X_1	X_1	X_1	X_2	X_2	X_2	X_1	
material costs	X_2	X_1	X_1	X_1	X_2	X_2	X_2	X_1	
logistics costs		X_1	X_1	X_1				X_1	
cost of capital		X_2	X_2	X_2				X_2	
environmental charges		X_2	X_2	X_2	X_3	X_2	X_2	X_2	
taxes and duties	X_2	X_2	X_2	X_2	X_3	X_2	X_2	X_2	
risk dependance on imports		X_2		X_2				X_2	
dependance on climate		X_1	X_1	X_1				X_1	
political instability		X_2		X_1	X_2	X_2	X_2	X_1	
strikes	X_1	X_2		X_1	X_1	X_1	X_1	X_1	
economic instability	X_1	X_2		X_1	X_1	X_1	X_1	X_1	
no possibility to use substitute material					X_2	X_2	X_2		
raw material speculations			X_2	X_2				X_2	

Illustration 79: Selecting market information

4.714 Gathering Information

Illustration 80 shows a possible structure for deciding how and where relevant information is to be collected.

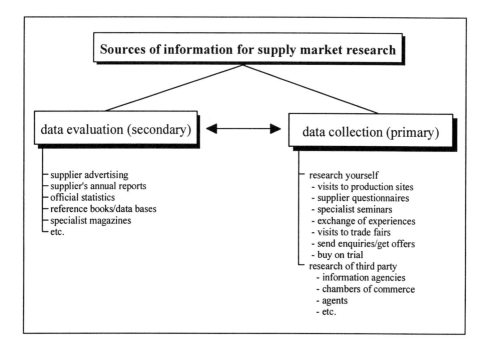

Illustration 80: Sources of information in supply market research

In daily business you will probably refer to secondary sources first. Looking for and interpreting existing material tends to be cheaper than referring to primary sources because this does not cause any actual research costs. However, more specific and detailed information can usually be gathered from primary sources.

The next question to be addressed is the suitability of the sources of information available to you. Illustration 81 shows that the suitability of these sources depends on what kind of information is required, with x_1 indicating high suitability and x_2 low suitability of a source.

Illustration 81 table — Sources of information about supplier performances.

Information about supplier performances		supplier advertising	supplier's annual report	specialist magazines	official statistics	reference books / data bases	supplier questionnaire	enquiries / offers	tours of production site	trade fairs	information agencies	agents	chamber of commerce	specialist seminars	orders on trial	etc.
quantity information	large quantity	X_5	X_4			X_4	X_1	X_2	X_1	X_3	X_2	X_4		X_2		
	small quantity	X_3	X_4			X_2	X_1	X_1	X_2	X_2	X_3	X_3	X_3	X_1		
	high significance of quantity	X_5	X_4				X_1	X_1		X_2				X_2		
	high quantity consistency						X_1	X_2		X_2				X_1		
performance information	acceptance of design methods		X_4				X_1	X_2		X_3		X_3		X_2	X_1	
	acceptance of design performances														X_1	
	adjustability of design methods	X_3	X_4				X_1	X_3	X_2	X_2				X_1		
	adjustability of performances							X_4	X_3	X_3				X_2	X_1	
	long life	X_4		X_3			X_1		X_1	X_3		X_2		X_1		
	performance consistency	X_3	X_4	X_3			X_1		X_1	X_3		X_2		X_1		
	application flexibility	X_2					X_1			X_2				X_3	X_2	
	visibility of performance	X_1	X_3				X_2		X_1	X_1				X_3	X_1	
	technological state-of-the-art	X_4	X_3	X_5		X_5	X_2	X_5	X_1	X_3	X_4	X_3		X_2	X_2	
	ability to manufacture tools	X_4	X_5			X_5	X_2	X_3	X_2	X_3	X_4	X_2		X_1	X_2	
	provisioning of tools and materials						X_1	X_1		X_3				X_2	X_1	
time information	short development time						X_2	X_2		X_3		X_2		X_1	X_1	
	short production time		X_4				X_2	X_2	X_2	X_3		X_2		X_1	X_1	
	short delivery time		X_4				X_2	X_2		X_3		X_2		X_1	X_1	
	provisioning of materials in time										X_3			X_1	X_1	
	observation of delivery data										X_3			X_1	X_1	
	flexible scheduling						X_1	X_3		X_2				X_1		
location information	easy access to storage facilities						X_1	X_2	X_1	X_2		X_2		X_2		
	transport links / infrastructure		X_4				X_1	X_2	X_1	X_2		X_2		X_2		
	acceptance of place of delivery						X_1	X_1		X_2		X_3	X_3	X_2		
delivery information	supplier reliability	X_3	X_4				X_2	X_3		X_3		X_2		X_1	X_1	
	packaging and transport protection		X_5	X_4			X_1	X_1		X_3		X_3		X_2	X_1	
	deliver materials ready for production		X_5	X_4			X_1	X_1	X_1	X_2		X_2		X_1	X_1	
	top priority of orders						X_1	X_2		X_3						
	exclusive rights			X_3			X_1	X_2		X_3		X_2		X_2		
	supplier security		X_2			X_3	X_1	X_1		X_3	X_2	X_2		X_3		
remuneration information	willingness to analyse costs						X_1	X_1		X_2		X_1		X_2		
	price security						X_2	X_2						X_1		
	longer payment periods						X_1	X_1				X_2		X_2		
	leasing option						X_1	X_1				X_2				
	performance-related discount						X_1	X_1								
	no charges for small orders						X_1	X_1								
service information	after-sales-service	X_2	X_3				X_1	X_1		X_2	X_3	X_2	X_2	X_2		
	recycling option	X_2	X_3	X_3			X_1	X_1		X_2		X_2		X_2	X_1	
	extended object guarantee						X_1	X_3	X_2	X_3		X_2		X_2	X_1	
	guaranteed follow-up orders						X_1	X_3		X_3		X_2		X_2		
	service capacity	X_2	X_3				X_1	X_1						X_2		
Information	information competence	X_3		X_3			X_2	X_2		X_2		X_2		X_1		
	willingness to provide information	X_2		X_3			X_1	X_2		X_2		X_2		X_1		
	willingness to solve problems	X_2	X_4				X_2	X_2		X_2		X_2		X_1	X_1	
	confidentiality	X_3					X_1	X_1		X_2				X_1		
	market information	X_2					X_1	X_1		X_2				X_1		
	application consulting	X_2	X_4	X_4			X_1	X_1		X_2		X_2		X_1		
	marketing cooperation	X_2					X_1	X_1		X_2						

Illustration 81: Sources of information about supplier performances

Information about supplier performances		supplier advertising	supplier's annual report	specialist magazines	official statistics	reference books / data bases	supplier questionnaire	enquiries / offers	tours of production site	trade fairs	information agencies	agents	chamber of commerce	specialist seminars	orders on trial	etc.
sales requirements	mutual growth						X_1			X_3			X_2			
	mutual qualification						X_1			X_3			X_2			
	opening of new markets						X_1			X_3			X_2			
	aquisition support						X_1			X_3			X_2			
	spare parts business						X_1			X_3			X_2			
	after-sales business done by purchaser						X_1			X_3			X_2			
	early information						X_1			X_3			X_2			
	etc.															
R+D/construction requirements	more know-how						X_1		X_2	X_3			X_2			
	usage of development potential						X_1			X_3			X_2			
	usage of new techniques						X_1		X_2	X_3			X_2			
	updating of know-how						X_1		X_2	X_3			X_2			
	exact instructions						X_1			X_3			X_2			
	open information flow						X_1			X_3			X_2			
	etc.															
production requirements	large production lots						X_1		X_2	X_3			X_2			
	long-term production						X_1		X_2	X_3			X_2			
	continous production						X_1	X_1	X_2	X_3			X_2			
	usage of idle production facilities						X_1		X_2	X_3			X_2			
	planning support						X_1		X_2	X_3			X_2			
	realization support						X_1		X_2	X_3			X_2			
	etc.															
supply requirements	opening of new supply markets						X_1			X_3			X_2			
	support in search for new suppliers						X_1			X_3			X_2			
	benefit from customers agreements withs.						X_1			X_3			X_2			
	training of purchasing stuff						X_1						X_2			
financial requirements	credits						X_1			X_3			X_2			
	early payment						X_1	X_1		X_3			X_2			
	higher payment security						X_1			X_3			X_2			
	fair pricing						X_1			X_3			X_2			
	bonus for special performances						X_1	X_1		X_3			X_2			
	etc.															
logistical requirements	readiness and tolerance when accepting deliveries						X_1			X_3			X_2			
	delivery to few sites						X_1	X_1		X_3			X_2			
	early and comprehensive information						X_1			X_3			X_2			
	support in establishing information system						X_1			X_3			X_2			
	etc.															
waste disposal req.	mutual planning of waste disposal						X_1			X_2			X_2			
	separation of materials						X_1	X_1		X_2			X_2			
	construction planning with a view to waste disposal						X_1						X_2			
	etc.															

Illustration 82: Sources of information about supplier requirements

154

It goes without saying that supplier questionnaires, requests for quotations, visits to trade fairs, audits and tours of your supplier's production sites as well as the participation in specialized conferences and seminars are particularly important and effective ways of gathering information.

The number of suitable sources of information is much more limited, however, when it comes to collecting information on the requirements of your suppliers.Illustration 82 indicates clearly that there are only few sources which can provide information on the requirements of your suppliers, the most effective of which is probably the supplier himself (supplier negotiations, supplier questionnaires). Exchanging information with your colleagues can be another way for securing important input, however, be aware not to overestimate that kind of information. Your internal or external sources might have made their experiences in a completely different demand situation. Time pressure tends to be a problem at trade fairs and time for discussions with a supplier about his plans and targets is usually limited. Audits and tours of your suppliers' sites allow you to realize what might be possible incentives for your supplier. Your impressions can either confirm what you have learned in conversations with your supplier or raise important questions. When analysing and comparing your suppliers' offers you also may be able to conclude what is important to them.

Illustration 83 shows possible sources of information about markets.

	Information sources → Market information about ↓	supplier advertising	supplier's annual report	specialist magazines	official statistics	reference books / data bases	supplier questionnaire	enquiries / offers	tours of production site	trade fairs	information agencies	agents	chamber of commerce	specialist seminars	trial orders	etc.
Performance	work performance					X_3					X_2	X_1	X_2			
	management performance										X_2	X_1	X_3			
	technology					X_2					X_2	X_1	X_2			
	logistical performance										X_2	X_1	X_2			
	communication performance										X_2	X_1	X_2			
	capital performance										X_2	X_1	X_2			
	national economics					X_2					X_2	X_1	X_2			
Cost	labour costs				X_1	X_1					X_1	X_2	X_1			
	material costs				X_1	X_1					X_1	X_2	X_1			
	logistical costs				X_1	X_1					X_1	X_2	X_1			
	cost of capital				X_1	X_1					X_1	X_2	X_1			
	environmental charges				X_3	X_2					X_1	X_1	X_2			
	taxes and duties				X_1	X_1					X_1	X_2	X_1			
Risk	dependance on imports				X_1	X_2					X_1	X_3	X_2			
	dependance on climate					X_2					X_1	X_1	X_2			
	political instability										X_1	X_1	X_2			
	strikes				X_2						X_1	X_1	X_2			
	economic instability				X_1	X_2					X_1	X_1	X_2			
	no possibility to use substitute material										X_1	X_2	X_2			
	raw material speculations										X_1	X_1	X_2			

Illustration 83: Sources of information about markets

The illustration indicates that, as far as markets are concerned, there are other sources of information which are of great importance and therefore used frequently. If you are looking into new markets you can obtain relevant information from special agencies, market research institutes, representations, chambers of commerce and, additionally, refer to business directories, trade reference books, special databases and official statistics.

If different sources of information are available to you, you can check which source offers the required information at the lowest cost. Illustration 84 classifies sources according to how reliable, up-to-date and cost-intensive the provided information is.

Suitability / Source of Information	high reliability		up-to-date aspect		low cost
	high security	high exactness	static	dynamic	
supplier advertising	o	-	+	-	+
supplier's annual report	o	o	-	-	+
specialist magazines	o	+	+	o	+
official statistics	+	o	-	-	+
reference books / database	+	o	-	-	+
supplier questionnaire	o	o	+	o	o
enquiries	+	+	+	o	o
vitits to production sites	+	+	+	o	o
visits to trade fairs	o	o	+	o	o
information agencies	o	o	o	o	-
agents	+	o	+	+	-
chambers of commerce	o	-	o	-	+
specialist seminars	+	+	+	o	-
trial orders	+	+	+	-	-

+ = requirement met fully   o = requirement met sufficiently   - = requirement not met satisfactorily

Illustration 84: Suitability of sources of information

In a specific corporate demand situations the purchasers involved have to decide which source of information is the most suitable, and why.

4.715 Processing and Presenting Information

We want to keep this chapter short as it deals with an issue which is not strictly the responsibility of procurement. Although we can certainly use statistical findings here, we can still ask which is the best way of processing and presenting the multitude of collected data in order to ensure that purchasers can actually refer to the data base and use the relevant information without much difficulty.

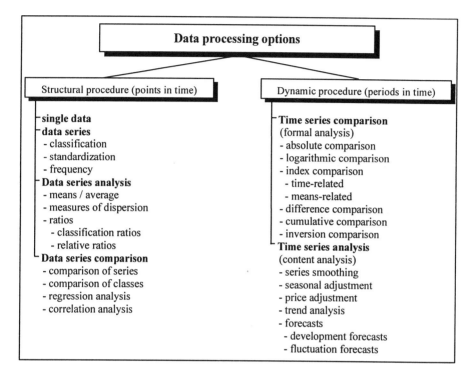

Illustration 85: Possible ways of processing information

Statistics can also provide us with a suitable way for presenting information as shown in Illustration 86. The overall target is to choose ways of presenting data which are short, transparent and yet informative.

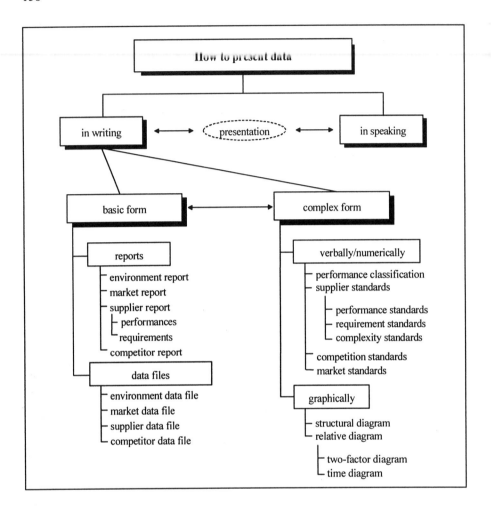

Illustration 86: Possible ways of presenting information

Information can be presented both in speaking and in writing. However, when presenting data orally you might still need something in writing to refer to. As the written presentation of information is transparent and always available for reference we want to focus on this option here. Basic forms of presenting data tend to show information in an isolated form. Much more valuable for the purchaser are more complex forms where a lot of information is presented on relatively little room. It depends on the company and the respective corporate situation which form of presentation is the most suitable. Frequent changes, however, which require that the user interprets data in different ways can be counterproductive.

4.72 Procurement Control

The management of a company through internal information is based on performance analyses conducted by all those involved in the manufacturing and procurement processes. Actual facts and figures are compared with target figures for the following purposes:

- As entrepreneurial activities are divided in planning, realization and control, performance analysis functions are required. Comparing actual facts and figures with target figures shows how effective corporate activities are.

- The leadership function of a company is based on the results of performance analyses. You can differenciate between the establishment of corporate objectives, the implementation of corporate objectives and the assurance of corporate objectives. According to Bleicher / Meyer (1976, p.56) assuring the achievement of corporate targets is the responsibility of a control function.

- When you realize that there is a discrepancy between targeted and actual results you have to check what kind of consequences this might have. An adjustment function has to decide whether special steps have to be taken to correct results. Both actual results (steps to be taken) and targeted results (redefining targets) can be adjusted.

- Steps are taken by people. Controls are there to manage what people do. Learning and motivation functions are of importance here. Actual results can show the acting person whether the set targets respectively the steps taken were right. Learning can mean to continue with the measures which have secured set targets in the past or to replace measures which failed to achieve the targeted results by more effective ones. Documented positive results can also increase staff motivation.

In addition to internal procurement control there has been an increasing trend to use *benchmarking* strategies for comparing processes in one procurement function with the ones in other companies. The main target is to compare your own performances with the best in the market. The optimum approach is to compare your function's performances with the absolute best even if the company with the "best practice" is actually in another line of business. Benchmarking in procurement is only just starting to become an issue.

160

4.721 The Control Process

Procurement control has three aspects: contents, methods and processes. Illustration 87 shows the different stages of the control process.

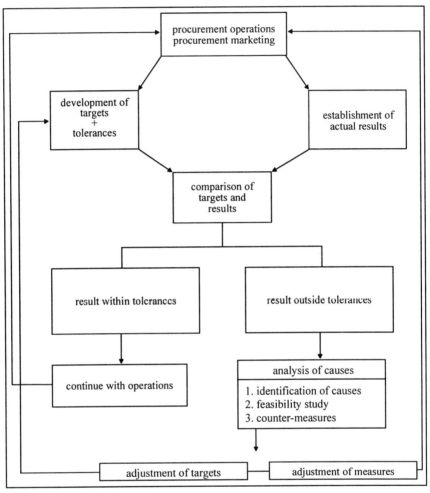

Illustration 87: Control process stages

From the marketing-oriented procurement approach described earlier we can deduct some necessary guidelines and benchmarks. It is important to define certain tolerances for establishing the limits in between which corporate results are "still acceptable". Deviations from targeted results which are still within these limits are to be treated as if the targeted result had actually been achieved. In such cases no adjustments are necessary in the respective procurement operations.

In case that the actual results are outside set limits, however, you have to check out systematically what might have caused the deviation and identify the causes clearly. There could be only one reason for the failure to achieve set targets or a whole boundle of reasons as well. In order to reduce the complexity of the latter, you should try to identify the central problem first.

After having established the causes of deviations (e.g. your supplier does nor have a quality assurance system) you have to work out what kind of possibilities you have to tackle the problem. Exchange rate fluctuations, for example, can hardly be dealt with in the short-term unless they have been anticipated beforehand and special steps (buying currency futures and options, change markets) have been taken to avoid the problem. It is important to see the supplier in his respective environment and, as it is difficult to influence the supplier's environment directly, to be ready to adjust to changing situations swiftly.

Once you have established that steps can be taken to harmonize actual situations with intended results you have to check the incentive-request quality of these steps, i.e. you have to work out at what cost (incentive) you can move actual results closer to intended results (request). When taking into account the economic principle you might find out that the planned steps are well worth the cost. Or you can conduct a value analysis in order to see whether it is your targets which need to be adjusted. This could mean setting targets a little bit lower or adjusting your materials planning.

This formal control process needs a focus.

4.722 Control Focus

What needs to be controlled? Selecting the "whats" equals setting targets. We have to take into account the economic principle again. You can set a lot of targets, but is it worth pursuing them? Let us concentrate on the adjustment function and thus on increasing corporate efficiency: Future operations are to secure set targets at minimum cost and expense. This is why procurement control should concentrate on such issues which have the potential to increase efficiency considerably.

162

In order to define the contents of control we can take another look at input-output processes. Control contents is input-oriented when the focus is on procurement instruments; it is output-oriented when its focus is on supply requirements. Moreover, it is
well worth examining to what extent procurement targets have actually been reached.
A few examples shall illustrate that in the following:

(1) Supply-oriented control contents

supply requirement	supply-related control ratios
quantity consistency	$\dfrac{\text{actual supply quantity x number of orders}}{\text{target orders}} \times 100$
usage flexibility	$\dfrac{\text{number of standardized objects}}{\text{total number of objects}} \times 100$
development / production / delivery time	$\dfrac{\text{quoted time}}{\text{requested time}} \times 100$
faithfulness to meet provisioning / delivery dates	$\dfrac{\text{number of delays}}{\text{number of deadlines}} \times 100$
flexible scheduling	$\dfrac{\text{number of changes in schedules}}{\text{number of agreed changes}} \times 100$
reliability in delivery	$\dfrac{\text{number of insufficient deliveries (quantity / time / place / quality)}}{\text{total number of deliveries}} \times 100$
packaging and transport protection	$\dfrac{\text{number of damaged objects}}{\text{total number of delivered objects}} \times 100$

Illustration 88 (1): Supply-oriented control ratios

cost analysis	supply-related control ratios
cost analysis	$\dfrac{\text{realized target costs}}{\text{required target costs}} \times 100$ → target cost realization quota
price security	$\dfrac{\varnothing \text{ cost price per reported period}}{\varnothing \text{ cost price per overall period}} \times 100$ per country / procurement object
	$\dfrac{\text{reduced purchase prices}}{\text{cost reduction realized with supplier}} \times 100$ → profitability quota
customer service	$\dfrac{\text{number of customer services realized to full satisfaction}}{\text{number of requested customer services}} \times 100$
recycling	$\dfrac{\text{quantity of replaceable waste material per materials category}}{\text{total quantity of waste material per materials category}} \times 100$ → substitution quota

Illustration 88 (2): Supply-oriented control ratios

supply requirement	supply-related control ratios
recycling	$\dfrac{\text{quantity of recycleable material per materials category}}{\text{total quantity of used material per materials category}} \times 100$ → recycling quota
	$\dfrac{\text{quantity / number of hazardous material}}{\text{total quantity of waste material}} \times 100$ → hazardous material quota
	$\dfrac{\text{quantity / number of reuseable material}}{\text{total quantity of useable material}} \times 100$ → reuseable materials quota
extended object guarantees and warrenties	$\dfrac{\text{granted extension of guarantees / warrenties (in months)}}{\text{targeted extension of guarantees / warrenties (in months)}} \times 100$
security of follow-up purchases (future availability of objects)	$\dfrac{\text{granted period for follow-up purchases (in years)}}{\text{targeted period for follow-up purchases (in years)}} \times 100$
service capacity	$\dfrac{\text{granted service capacity}}{\text{targeted service capacities (storage, development, testing, etc.)}} \times 100$

Illustration 88 (3): Supply-oriented control ratios

Some supply requirements described in chapter 4.22 have been allocated to control ratios (as quotas). In order to control whatever is important in a concrete demand situation you will have to select those possibilities from Illustration 36 which relate to the specific if-conditions required by your company .

In addition to controlling the fulfillment of requirements you can control the creation of requirements. Thus you can check whether you have acted in accordance with your procurement targets when you identified your supply requirements or whether mistake were made.

(2) Instrument-oriented control contents

Illustration 22 was an overview of concrete procurement targets. This overview is the basis for the control ratios (in quotas) shown in Illustration 89.

some instrumental targets	instrumental target-related control ratios
market presence	$\frac{\text{No. of used markets for all objects / specific objects}}{\text{No. of possible markets for all objects / specific objects}}$
exclusive rights quota	$\frac{\text{exclusive suppliers}}{\Sigma \text{ No. of suppliers}} \times 100$
purchasing cooperation	$\frac{\text{No. of realized cooperations}}{\text{No. of possible cooperations}}$ $\frac{\text{cooperation purchasing volume}}{\Sigma \text{ purchasing volume}} \times 100$
readiness to deliver	$\frac{\text{No. of prompt deliveries}}{\Sigma \text{ No. of requested deliveries}}$
price reduction quota	$\frac{\text{realized object price reductions}}{\text{market price (index)}}$
fixed price quota	$\frac{\text{No. of fixed price agreements per term}}{\text{all object prices per term}}$
price quota (own currency)	$\frac{\text{No. of supply contracts in x currency}}{\Sigma \text{ supply contracts}}$

Illustration 89: Instrument-oriented control ratios

(3) Procurement target-oriented control contents

By using the control key figures illustrated in the following we want to focus on some of the most important procurement targets:

- reduction of supply costs,
- reduction of supply risks,
- increase of supply quality,
- increase of supply flexibility.

Other aspects, as important as they may be, cannot be examined here. The following figures are for classification and future reference.

When looking at the figures you will see that some control ratios are used several times. The standardization quota, for example, is used for supply requirements and a variety of procurement targets such as cost reduction, increased supply security and increased flexibility. The activities on which these ratios are based can lead to different results. If you standardize parts, for example, you may be able to use them for different products; due to standardization projects quantities might increase, thus leading to cost degression; as standard parts are usually supplied by several sources, the security of supply increases; increasing the number of possibilities for using a part increases adjustment flexibility. Illustration 90 (1 - 3) shows some examples.

funct-ional target	functional target-related control ratios		
increase in quality	deficiency complaint quota	=	$\dfrac{\text{number of deficient objects}}{\Sigma \text{ number of delivered objects}} \times 100$ → per supplier, plant, country, etc.
	delivery complaint quota	=	$\dfrac{\text{number of complaints about deliveries}}{\Sigma \text{ number of deliveries}} \times 100$ → per supplier, plant, country. etc.
	service complaint quota	=	$\dfrac{\text{number of complaints about services}}{\Sigma \text{ number of services renderd}} \times 100$ → per supplier
	damage complaint quota	=	$\dfrac{\text{number / value of damaged deliveries}}{\Sigma \text{ number of delivered objects}} \times 100$ → per supplier
	waste disposal problem quota	=	$\dfrac{\text{number of complaints about waste disposal}}{\Sigma \text{ quantity of disposed waste}} \times 100$
	delay in delivery quota	=	$\dfrac{\text{number of delays}}{\Sigma \text{ number of deliveries}}$
	parts missing quota	=	$\dfrac{\text{number of deliveries with parts missing}}{\Sigma \text{ number of deliveries}}$
	framework agreement quota	=	$\dfrac{\text{purchasing volume in framework agreement}}{\Sigma \text{ purchasing}} \times 100$

Illustration 90 (1): Procurement target-oriented ratios

funct-ional target	functional target-related control ratios		
cost reduction	cost reduction quota total / partial	$=$	$\dfrac{\text{reduction of this year's purchasing volume in \% (total / partial)}}{\text{last year's purchasing volume (total / partial)}} \times 100$
	∅ purchasing volume	$=$	$\dfrac{\text{purchasing volume in \% (total / per member of staff)}}{\text{numbers of orders (total / per member of staff)}}$
	travel expense quota	$=$	$\dfrac{\text{travel expense}}{\text{number of purchasing staff}} \times 100$
	information cost quota	$=$	$\dfrac{\Sigma\text{ information cost (trade fairs, travel, data banks, etc.)}}{\Sigma \text{ procurement costs / purchasing volume}} \times 100$
	usage deviation quota	$=$	$\dfrac{\text{actual materials usage}}{\text{projected materials usage}} \times 100$
	procurement cost quota	$=$	$\dfrac{\Sigma \text{ procurement costs}}{\text{net turnover}} \times 100$
	purchasing volume quota	$=$	$\dfrac{\text{purchasing volume}}{\text{net turnover}} \times 100$
	∅ costs per order	$=$	→ reduction of average costs per order Σ $\dfrac{\text{total costs of orders}}{\text{total numbers of orders}}$ per department per product per member of staff per framework agreement
	∅ order value	$=$	→ increase of order value $\dfrac{\text{purchasing volume}}{\text{total number of orders}}$
	order structure / order value class	$=$	$\dfrac{\varnothing \text{ order value}}{\text{purchasing volume}}$

Illustration 90 (2): Procurement target-oriented ratios

funct-ional target	functional target-related control ratios		
cost reduction	⌀ storage time	=	→ reduction of stock-keeping costs $\dfrac{\text{inventory level x 240 days}}{\text{annual usage}}$
	SCQ	=	→ reduction of the short notice cost quota (SCQ) $\dfrac{\Sigma \text{ cost of short notice deliveries per function}}{\Sigma \text{ procurement costs per function}}$
	MCQ	=	→ reduction of missing materials cost quota (MCQ) $\dfrac{\text{cost of stopping production}}{\text{production costs}}$ x 100
	standardization quota (including variability)	=	$\dfrac{\text{number of standardized purchasing objects}}{\Sigma \text{ number of procurement objects}}$ x 100
	offer / enquiry quota	=	$\dfrac{\text{number of enquiries / offers}}{\text{order volume (processes)}}$ x 100
		=	$\dfrac{\text{enquiries / offers}}{\text{purchasers / members of staff}}$
		=	$\dfrac{\text{orders}}{\text{enquiries}}$ x 100
	volume quota	=	$\dfrac{\text{purchasing volume (procurement objects)}}{\Sigma \text{ purchasing volume (material)}}$ x 100
	storage quota	=	$\dfrac{\Sigma \text{ inventory level per procurement object}}{\Sigma \text{ net turnover / purchasing volume}}$ x 100

Illustration 90 (3): Procurement target-oriented ratios

funct-ional target	functional target-related control ratios	
increase in security	inventory range $=$	$$\dfrac{\text{inventory level on target day}}{\varnothing \text{ usage per day / month}}$$ $$\dfrac{\text{inventory level + ordered material}}{\text{projected usage per day}}$$
	inventory structure $=$	$$\dfrac{\text{inventory level of sensitive procurement objects}}{\text{overall inventory level}}$$
	established supplier quota $=$	$$\dfrac{\text{purchasing volume with established suppliers per period}}{\text{total purchasing volume}} \times 100$$
	standardization quota $=$	$$\dfrac{\text{number of standardized procurement objects}}{\Sigma \ \text{number of deliveries}} \times 100$$
	missing / non-delivery quota $=$	$$\dfrac{\text{number of missing / non-deliveries}}{\Sigma \ \text{number of deliveries}} \times 100$$
	regional market quota $=$	$$\dfrac{\text{purchasing volume in regional markets}}{\Sigma \ \text{total purchasing}} \times 100$$
	sensitivity quota $=$	$$\dfrac{\text{number / volume of sensitive procurement objects}}{\Sigma \ \text{number / volume of procurement objects}} \times 100$$
	substitution quota $=$	$$\dfrac{\text{number of replaceable sensitive procurement objects}}{\Sigma \ \text{number of sensitive procurement objects}} \times 100$$

Illustration 90 (4): Procurement target-oriented ratios

170

funct-ional target	functional target-related control ratios		
cost reduction	⊘ storage time	=	→ reduction of stock-keeping costs $\dfrac{\text{inventory level x 240 days}}{\text{annual usage}}$
	SCQ	=	→ reduction of the short notice cost quota (SCQ) $\dfrac{\Sigma \text{ cost of short notice deliveries per function}}{\Sigma \text{ procurement costs per function}}$
	MCQ	=	→ reduction of missing materials cost quota (MCQ) $\dfrac{\text{cost of stopping production}}{\text{production costs}} \times 100$
	standardization quota (including variability)	=	$\dfrac{\text{number of standardized purchasing objects}}{\Sigma \text{ number of procurement objects}} \times 100$
	offer / enquiry quota	=	$\dfrac{\text{number of enquiries / offers}}{\text{order volume (processes)}} \times 100$
		=	$\dfrac{\text{enquiries / offers}}{\text{purchasers / members of staff}}$
		=	$\dfrac{\text{orders}}{\text{enquiries}} \times 100$
	volume quota	=	$\dfrac{\text{purchasing volume (procurement objects)}}{\Sigma \text{ purchasing volume (material)}} \times 100$
	storage quota	=	$\dfrac{\Sigma \text{ inventory level per procurement object}}{\Sigma \text{ net turnover / purchasing volume}} \times 100$

Illustration 90 (5): Procurement target-oriented ratios

4.723 Control Methods

How can we describe intended results in a way that ensures that we can measure them as well? Generally, we can refer to the qualities objectivity, validity and reliability. Both actual and intended supply requirements should be defined in a way which avoids any emotional exaggerations and secures objectivity. The key figures for measuring control contents have to be adequate and valid. Content validity tends to be difficult to achieve at first and is prone to cause discussions, but it puts an important focus on what is really important. Realibility is important to make sure that no mistakes are made in measuring performances. Detailed measuring instructions are required here.

Control can be effected through scale analysis or ratio analysis.

(1) *Scale analysis* allows to set up uniform control figures based on exact data (see Pfisterer 1988, p.86, 92 pp). There are different kinds of scales:
- nominal scales based on decisions (yes / no)
- ordinal scales based on ratings (larger / smaller)
- cardinal scales based on specified intervalls

Many supply requirements can be controlled with nominal scales while markets and suppliers should be assessed with ordinal scales. For our tasks ratios and benchmarks seem more suitable than cardinal scales.

(2) *Ratios or benchmarks* can be used to create a transparent and valuable number system which reflects economic facts in a highly concentrated form. Such number systems are the basis for *benchmarking* strategies as well. Pfisterer (1988, p. 88, and literature indicated therein) favoured the structure shown in Illustration 91.

172

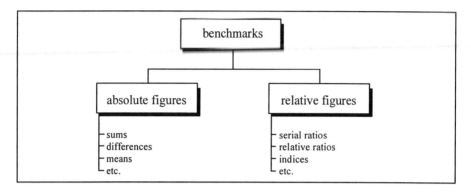

Illustration 91: Types of ratios /benchmarks

The annual purchasing volume per department, employee, supplier etc. is character-ized by fluctuations in quantity and time (e.g. budget deviations, actual figures - target figures). Provided that the business environment has not undergone major changes, this reflects the quality of planning and / or of the procurement steps that were taken. You can, for example, establish the average price of a procurement object mathemati-cally. Such absolute figures, however, do not suffice to ensure efficient procurement control.

We are more interested in relative ratios. When using classification figures we com-pare a subset with a total set over the same period of time. If you multiply this subset with 100 you get its share of the total set. When you use relative figures, you compare figures which are essentially different but have been put in relation to one another for a certain period of time. By using indices (rather than the number 100) you can estab-lish whether there have been any fluctuations over that period of time.

We have sought to develop ratios for classification which relate to different supply as-pects discussed in the present book.

Pfisterer (1988, p. 97) developed a scheme for the interaction of control methods as shown in Illustration 92.

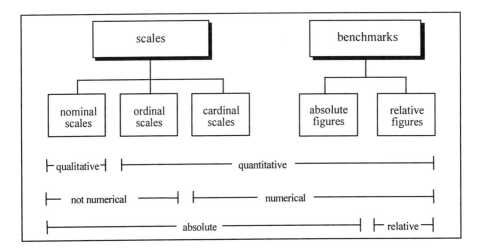

Illustration 92: Interaction between control methods

The last question that needs to be addressed is where to obtain the required data for creating number systems from. Here you can refer to your in-house documentation and computer systems. The more you use computers to support decision-making processes in procurement, the more actual and target data you will gather over the time. Your in-house computer system can provide you with relevant data from other corporate functions such as finance, accounting, statistics, etc.

Thus the chain of procurement marketing processes has come full circle.

List of Illustrations

176

Literature

- Ansoff, I. A Model for Diversification, in: Management Science 1958
- Arnold, U.: Beschaffungsinformation, in: HWD, book 1, 5th edition, published by v.W. Wittelmann et al., Stuttgart 1993
- Arnold, U.: Beschaffungsmanagement
- Berndt, R.: Total Quality Management als Erfolgsstrategie, Heidelberg 1995
- Biergans, B.: Zur Entwicklung eines marketingadäquaten Ansatzes und Instrumentariums für die Beschaffung, book 1 of the series "Beiträge zum Beschaffungsmarketing", published by U. Koppelmann, Cologne 1984
- Bleicher, K./ Meyer, E.: Führung in der Unternehmung, Reinbeck bei Hamburg 1976
- Cynert R.M./March J.G.: A Behavioral Theory of the Firm, Englewood Cliffs 1963
- Endler, D.: Produktteile als Mittel der Produktgestaltung, book 21 of the series "Beiträge zum Beschaffungsmarketing", published by U. Koppelmann, Cologne 1992
- Gutenberg, E.: Grundlagen der Betriebswirtschaftslehre, book 1, 24th edition, Berlin 1983
- Hammer, R.: Unternehmensplanung, Munich 1982
- Hiromoto, T.: Management Accounting in Japan, in: Controlling, 1st year, No. 6, 1989
- Koppelmann, U.: Beschaffungsmarketing, 2nd edition, Heidelberg 1995
- Kopsidis, R.M. Materialwirtschaft: Grundlagen, Methoden, Techniken, Politik, 2nd edition, Munich/Vienna 1992
- Kotler, Ph.: A Generic Concept of Marketing, in: JM, Vol. 36, April 1972
- Kraljic, P.: Neue Wege im Beschaffungsmarketing, in MM, No.11, 1977
- Kreikebaum, H.: Strategische Unternehmensplannung, Stuttgart 1981
- March, J.G./Simon, H.A.: Organisation, New York 1958
- Meyer, C.: Beschaffungsziele, book 5 of the series "Beiträge zum Beschaffungsmarketing", published by U. Koppelmann, Cologne 1986

178

- Pfisterer, J.: Beschaffungskontrolle, book 7 of the series "Beiträge zum Beschaffungsmarketing", published by U. Koppelmann, Cologne 1990

- Porter, M.E.: Wettbewerbsvorteile, Frankfurt a. M./ New York 1986

- Raffée, H. Marketing und Umwelt, Stuttgart 1979

- Scherer, J.: Zur Entwicklung und zum Einsatz von Objektmerkmalen als Entscheidungskriterien in der Beschaffung, book 9 of the series "Beiträge zum Beschaffungsmarketing", published by U. Koppelmann, Cologne 1991

- Seidenschwarz, W. Target costing: marktorientiertes Zielkostenmanagement, Munich 1993

- Simon, H.A.: A Behavioral Model of Rational Choices, in: Quarterly Journal of Economics, 69 (February), 1995

- Stangl, U.: Beschaffungsmarktforschung - Ein heuristisches Entscheidungsmodell, book 2 of the series "Beiträge zum Beschaffungsmarketing", published by U. Koppelmann, Cologne 1985

- Theisen, P.: Grundzüge einer Theorie der Beschaffungspolitik, Berlin 1970

- without named author: Industrieller Einkauf heute, Beschaffung aktuell, 12/95, p. 25

Index

Printing: Druckhaus Beltz, Hemsbach
Binding: Buchbinderei Schäffer, Grünstadt